PAYING the PRICE

Simon Feldman
with Krisztina Javor

We are deeply grateful to our families, friends and all those who have stood by us - through every chapter of our lives and throughout the creation of this book. Your encouragement, love and support has been a constant source of inspiration and your belief motivated us every step of the way.

Paying the Price
IPaperback: ISBN: 9781761099045
eBook: ISBN: 9781740273855
Copyright © text Simon Feldman & Krisztina Javor 2025
Copyright © cover photography: Iris Nieri & Michael Bulla
Cover design by Graham Davidson
In the interest of privacy and confidentiality, some names and identifying details in this memoir have been changed.

First published 2025 by
Ginninderra Press
PO Box 2 Bentleigh 3204
www.ginninderrapress.com.au

Praise for Paying the Price

Simon Feldman has not only wiped the slate clean - his book is a vivid, well written manual for dealing with life in prison. It should be compulsory reading for the misfortunate facing the bruised fruits of their mistakes. Humble, realistic, empathetic, embracing the crime, and writing his truth in graphic prose and poetry.

Charles C. Waterstreet,
Theatre and film producer,
author and former barrister

Feldman's words are haunting. His remorse and shame slowly give way to insight and self-compassion. The path following his release from jail is littered with exhausting attempts to achieve redemption, and setbacks that see him imprisoned in new ways. In his own words, 'the real work is only just beginning'.

Jo Lamble,
Clinical Psychologist
and author

I have done many fraud cases and thousands of pro bono hours supporting people and families with a mental illness. The chapter regarding the dissociative fugue really hit home, as the real price paid from years of trauma. So, thank you for having the courage to write this book. It's a very important piece on life after conviction and whether, as a society, we are at all interested in rehabilitation.

David Leggatt,
Lawyer & Director, BlueRock Law

Contents

Guilty Verdict	7
Day 1 Dawn de Loas Correctional Centre	11
Jail Classification	15
Fairy Godfather	17
Little Jimmy	21
The Boneyard	25
The Librarian	27
The Bank Robber and the Boxer	32
Haircuts and Captain America	36
Mobile Phones and Contraband	39
The Sweeper	43
Justice Health	46
C3, With Leave	50
Work Release For a Living	54
Attila My Mum	59
Grateful Groundhog Day	63
Back at the Kitchen (OBK)	66
Yard Culture	71
Jail Ingenuity	74
The Ambush	77
Missing Clues	81
Programs	86
Inmate Delegate Committee (IDC)	89
Debt and the Gamble	92
The Daily Blue	95
Civil Proceedings	100
Moving On	106
The Sword of Damocles	110
Segro	114

The Real Rake	119
Due Process	122
Sentencing	125
Visits	128
The Primal Urge	132
Is Anyone Spared, I Wonder	136
Tyre Kickers	139
Choices	143
Keep On Digging	146
King Richard	149
WTF	152
A Fortunate Boy	154
Israel	158
Life in San Francisco	162
Back in Perth	169
Move to Sydney	172
Mr Steele Abroad	176
Working-class Man	179
The Circle of Life	183
The Hardest Day	186
One Step at a Time	188
Phoenix Rising Perhaps	190
Becoming a Father Again	193
Setbacks	198
And Life Goes On	204
Friend or Foe	208
Mirror Mirror	211

Guilty Verdict

I stood frozen in the dock, my head exploding as I grappled with absorbing the sentence the judge had just imposed. My eyes were fixated on my barrister to guide me and interpret what the judgement meant. As he placed his hand on my shoulder, I sensed that this gentle gesture was loaded with an overwhelming weight. In a dry matter of fact tone he stated, 'Simon we did OK, that's four years minimum jail time for you.'

I turned around to look at my family and friends who had come to support me in court, holding on to each other in alarm. The court's corrective services officer allowed me to say farewell to them and then led me downstairs to the cells. He took my watch, wallet, chain, glasses and all the possessions that I had with me and, of course, my belt and shoelaces. As I later learnt, the belt and laces were to protect me from self-harm. And so I was placed in what is known in jail speak as 'an escort truck', to take my first ride as a sentenced inmate. My first jolt into jail life also included being double-cuffed, meaning that I was in handcuffs and also cuffed to the escort truck.

The truck moved out of the court cells of Downing Centre, for the familiar 500-metre journey to the esoteric

Correctional Services-run Surry Hills Cells, hoping to avoid the ever-present media. It would be my second visit to this underground hellhole and to this day, I remain convinced that it exists to simply break its population. In theory, the Cells are supposed to be a twenty-four-hour holding area until a suitable corrective centre can be found, but in reality, it is where both remand and sentenced inmates are degraded over an extended period. As was the case on both of my visits, I was placed in a large concrete room alone, with nothing other than a concrete bench as a bed, an overflowing toilet bowl and a sink. There was a television blasting non-stop at full volume and the flickering fluorescent light was on day and night. The place was rat-infested and the smell of human faeces was sickening. Keeping me company were also the constant screams of drug addicts going cold turkey and alcoholics drying out in surrounding cells.

From the moment I got out of the escort truck, and for the next four years, I was no longer Simon Feldman. I was now known as 466897, the MIN (master index number) assigned to me. It effectively dehumanises the person, because along with losing your name you of course also lose your freedom, your dignity and all the rights that one would normally take for granted. This so-called burden of institutionalisation often stays with inmates who have done a significant jail term and will likely forever haunt them.

This, being my second time around, I was prepared for the inevitable strip search. In a room, alone with two male officers, I stood naked and bent over and every part of me was searched for any contraband. Once you are convicted, the tone with which you are unexpectedly spoken to and the contempt that you are treated with pretty quickly jolts you to the reality that you are now persona non grata.

In this holding facility, communication with the outside world is limited to one phone call, regardless of the length of stay. The timing and length of the call is purely at the discretion of the corrective services officers. In fact, pretty soon you come to feel as if your entire existence is at their discretion. You quickly come to understand why these officers are universally called 'screws' by those in green.

For many Sydney-siders, Hyde Park offers beauty and peace for a leisurely walk. But if one looks at the ground during their visit, they may notice beautiful, decorative glass bricks. I imagine that very few know that the shadows they may observe underneath the thick glass are those of inmates naked and showering while watching the world go by. Just another reminder of the price of their crime. Each day, we were led to this cold, concrete mass shower and stayed until the hot water ran out, generally a couple of minutes. And then with no towels provided, marched back to the concrete cell.

I spent the next seven days in the same clothes that I fronted court in. The clothes on my back served as my blanket, towel and pillow. After the first couple of days, I lost track of the time and, I'm pretty certain, reality too. I was overcome with a complete sense of helplessness and hopelessness, overwhelmed with being utterly alone, not to mention without purpose and significance in life. I remember being in a foetal position on the cold floor absolutely freezing, shaking and crying uncontrollably. Surviving four years like this seemed totally unimaginable.

I have no concept of how many times I broke down and curled up in a ball wishing to die. My entire being wanted to shut down but couldn't. I wanted to give up and simply couldn't imagine tomorrow. My mind would not, could not, quieten. It was relentlessly racing, ruminating and taunting me about the journey that led me to this point. The moment I was caught, I did not hesitate owning up to my crime. I embezzled $16.64 million. A careless oversight that turned into a mountain of deception. How it started, why it started and why it continued is irrelevant now. What matters is that I did not choose the right path at any stage. My god, why didn't I? And now it was too late, it was penance time and not only in the eyes of the law. Life leading up to this point was noisy and often hell. It's now quiet, however. What's left is all the time in the world for me to face me.

The internal dialogue of self-hate, disdain and disappointment was crushing, but the guilt of the shame and pain I had brought on my three young children, family and loved ones simply broke me.

Day 1 Dawn de Loas Correctional Centre

The Silverwater Correctional Complex has four different sections consisting of a jail for men, a jail for women, the Dawn de Loas Correctional Centre and the Metropolitan Remand and Reception Centre (MRRC), which is a maximum-security facility and the largest of its kind in Australia.

I spent about a week at MRRC before being transferred to the Dawn de Loas Correctional Centre, my home for the next four years. The facility is divided into general population and protective custody and I was placed in the latter to serve my time. To my surprise, I felt a slight sense of relief as we pulled into Dawn de Loas, which, even at first glance, was a far cry from the cold and sterile environment of the MRRC. I could see gardens, a basketball court and what appeared to be housing units.

Reception is called the 'intake' and was a process of two officers inducting the new arrival to all the regulations of jail life. Just like the other jails that I had moved through, these officers were also familiar with who I was and my crime. In fact, one of the female officers even joked that she used to shop in one of my stores and proceeded to explain that this particular jail had been originally designed and built for pregnant women in custody. Some time later, I even saw a bath and birthing room in each wing. However, they were locked at all times, because privileges like a bath were unattainable in jail.

Part of the intake process was also signing a semi-formal contract agreeing to the inmate's code of conduct, which seemed somewhat ironic given that the common denominator to us all was having broken the law. I also signed for all my personal belongings to be locked in a secure locker for my entire stay and was then provided new jail greens which I changed into at once.

Two burly guards then led me through the intake gate through to the jail yard. I was fearfully walking behind the officers, wondering what on earth my world would look like from this point onward.

My initiation into the jail population occurred immediately upon arrival to the yard full of strangers also dressed in green. My journey to this point rendered me a hollow, grey-skinned, sixty-kilogram shell of my former self. Feeling somewhat protected by the presence of the guards, I looked out into the yard and observed countless eyes looking straight back, as if sizing me up like a fresh piece of meat. A sense of dread and fear was quickly coming over me, made worse by noticing an enormous human walking out of the crowd and making his way towards where the guards and I were standing. I was positioned at the top of three stairs overlooking the main prison yard as the giant approached. The two prison officers retreated almost as if in respect.

As he stopped at the bottom of the three steps, he was still easily my height. He looked me straight in the eyes and I think he was easily twice my weight too and his head was the size of a basketball. In a thick eastern European accent, his first words to me were "Are you an Aussie, boy?"

Frozen with fear and unsure what the correct response should be, I reluctantly replied, "Yes."

His immediate response as he stared me down was "Don't you lie to me, Jew boy."

I can't recall the exact thoughts that were racing through my mind at this time, but they included wondering if I would make it through the first day.

However, before I could even truly consider my fate any further, Kovaks, the Romanian drug lord, broke into a big, warm smile, put his arm around me in front of the entire yard and said, "Don't worry, Simon. I have been told to look after you."

Looking back, this was the first time I felt any semblance of safety in what seemed like for ever. Kovaks led me through the yard, arm around my shoulders, and at that point I knew that I would be safe and protected, in the short term at least. I later realised that it was my first lesson in how jail favours worked and that jail life is one big barter economy.

I am often asked about how I got through the first few nights of my sentence. How I slept, how I felt, what I thought about. To my amazement, my very first 'sleep' in jail was quite good. I had been on high alert during my entire time at the MRRC and hardly slept at all. Arriving to start my sentence offered respite from the chaos and the intensity of the weeks before and I suddenly felt a sense of certainty and a little peace. All very short-lived feelings of course. Before too long, for the next four years and even to this day, the 'Why the fuck did I do that?' is never too far from my mind.

Jail Classification

Within the NSW jail system, inmates are classified as a result of their crime, the severity and the length of their sentence. Their classification will also influence the correctional facility they will be assigned to. The process of classification is to start at a predetermined security level, the objective being to reduce the level of security as an inmate nears release date.

The highest classification is AA, reserved for terrorists – those considered as a danger not just to fellow inmates but to mankind itself. They are housed in what the general public would know as super max facilities. Maximum-security inmates are next and have an A classification, generally serving seven or more years as a minimum sentence. The next classification is B, assigned to medium-security inmates, serving around five to seven years as a minimum sentence. Minimum-security inmates, serving up to four and a half years or less are classified as C.

Both B and C classifications are broken down to B1 and B2, C1, C2 and C3, with C3 inmates having the lowest classification within the NSW jail system. The movement down the classification system is dependent on the inmate's behaviour and completion of all required rehabilitative courses to address the offending behaviour specific to their crime. Therefore, there are separate rehabilitation programs for sex offenders, alcoholics, violent offenders and drug users, to name a few.

Most inmates at the MRRC are unconvicted or unsentenced. All unsentenced inmates on remand in NSW are classified as A-Unsentenced, which means that they are technically maximum-security inmates until such time that they are sentenced. Therefore, depending on the charges that they are facing and the court's due process, on-remand inmates can be in MRRC for months or even years.

Fairy Godfather

The cost of surviving in jail is high. While three rationed meals, clothing and accommodation are provided, everything else has to be paid for by the inmate. When I arrived in jail, I was a little heartened to see an extensive grocery shopping list and a secondary list of household items. My excitement, however, was short-lived, as the possibility of acquiring any of these meant that I needed money each week in my jail account. Additional funds were necessary to supplement meals and also to purchase shoes, TV, kettle, toaster, doona, sweater or a fan, as none of them were free. In fact, the first lesson in jail is that nothing is free. It's great if the inmate can afford to pay for these crucial 'luxuries'. However, that failing, the barter economy of jail life becomes the only option, where the currency is doing favours for food and supplies.

Knowing that I had minimal funds in my jail account was of great concern. Despite the $13.50 per week I was being paid to be a jail gardener from the first day, it was not sufficient to adequately supplement jail food or to afford any basic comforts. Jail food is largely inedible and pretty much serves up Groundhog Day 365 days a year. Breakfast, dropped at six a.m., was half a loaf of bread, a bag of random cereal and a 300-millilitre carton of jail-prepared, watered-down milk. Lunch, dropped at eleven a.m., consisted of a rotation of faux meat or chicken sandwich and possibly a stale pastry. Dinner, 'served' at three thirty p.m., was always hot and was generally either runny lasagne, an unidentifiable meat dish or chicken leg, accompanied by vegetables. The chicken leg had to have been genetically modified, as it was the size of a lamb shank. I don't think I have ever seen a chicken that big.

Family and friends on the outside play a crucial role in the quality of your life in jail. Those who had people supplement jail life by putting money into their jail account were fortunate. And to my great surprise, Chaim, an old business colleague of mine, came to my aid. Despite the fact that he had lost money as a result of my financial improprieties, he never gave up on me or walked away and made it his mission to ensure that my jail account was full every week. The maximum weekly grocery buy-up amount was $65 when I arrived in jail and $85 a week by the time I left. Buy-up is a term for the weekly food items you could purchase. There was also a monthly buy-up, where one could purchase electrical and general items. Among other items, Chaim's support enabled me to buy as much tuna, as I needed which was the only form of protein available on the weekly buy-up list.

Not only did Chaim send me money every week but, without fail, he also visited me on the first Sunday of every month. During the visits, he would always offer to reach out and communicate with any family, friends, legal or pastoral contacts who might not be appropriate to converse with on my daily monitored phone calls. All phone calls in jail are monitored and recorded and can be a maximum six minutes long. One can make as many calls as they like, but it becomes very cost prohibitive. Each six-minute phone call cost $3, which meant you could burn through your jail funds very quickly.

The cost of groceries was equally steep, about one and a half times the cost of food on the outside. My weekly grocery items consisted of approximately twenty cans of tuna, twenty servings of one-minute rice, toiletries, two-minute noodles and a bag of Black & White chocolate chip cookies. I was quite surprised that after four years on this Mediterranean diet, I did not end up growing a dorsal fin. My weekly treat was a Cadbury Boost bar and the rest of my money went towards phone calls. To this day, when I walk past the canned fish while I am grocery shopping, I think of lunch or dinner. Needless to say, I don't ever buy tuna but am still OK to eat it.

As I am writing this book, sitting in a park situated on the harbour shore of Sydney's eastern suburbs, the weather is warm and there are many COVID lockdown picnics around us. People are preparing for the end of lockdown or 'freedom day', which is supposed to be one week away. As someone who has spent time in jail, I can't help but sneer a little when I hear people complain about COVID lockdown life in Sydney. If only people knew what real lockdown entailed. A place where there is no internet, no phone, a two by four metre cell for up to twenty-four hours a day, no family and no friends. It's just you, trying to get through one day at a time without harm, be it from other inmates or the games played by cruel jailers. And that's not even describing a hard lockdown. Hard lockdowns can be imposed due to staff shortage, an attempted escape, death in custody, a suspected dangerous contraband find by the screws, violence and, more often than not, union strike action. Hard lockdowns could last anywhere between one and three days and I think that I went through about thirty of them.

Needless to say, trying to recall and pen the stories of my jail life is very surreal. Even in the midst of Sydney's lockdown, it feels like I am telling the story of another person altogether, who between 2011 and 2015 was told when to eat, sleep and use the bathroom. And a person who during that time was totally beholden to the compassion of other people like Chaim.

Little Jimmy

About one year into my sentence, my first cellmate moved out and the officers asked if I was OK with having a man in his late twenties as my 'cellie' (slang for cell mate) and whether I could look out for him. He apparently had a good reputation in the yard and so I agreed. The harsh reality, however, was that I could have been given any random cell mate and the request was more of a heads up, but at least this one, Jimmy, seemed to check out.

In jail, seniority means that the oldest person in the cell gets the bottom bunk and the youngest sleeps at the top. Young Jimmy, however, asked me if he could have the bottom bunk as he didn't sleep well on the top. Given that my previous rooming rendered me the younger cell mate and I had just now moved to the bottom bunk, I was not willing to switch and told him no.

Each night after muster, the inmates were locked in their cell. Muster is the jail term for roll call or head count and happens daily at six a.m., ten thirty a.m. and six p.m., which is lock-in time. If an inmate missed a muster, there were consequences and possibly loss of privileges. At muster, your bed must always be made, you must be wearing shoes and dressed neatly.

On our first night in our cell, my new room-mate Jimmy decided to pull the mattress off the top bunk and sleep on the floor. Given that I had denied his request of the bottom bunk, I thought nothing of it, turned the lights out and prepared for sleep. In the middle of the night, however, I woke to a banging noise. At the time, I thought it was a general jail sound, but it didn't stop, becoming louder, more consistent, and seemed to be getting closer. I rolled over and couldn't see Jimmy on his mattress. I then turned the light on. I saw Jimmy standing in the shower cubicle of our cell, next to the bunk bed. He was banging his head against the concrete wall, with blood streaming down his split open skull, otherwise known as a 'crimson mask' in jail. I jumped up to see the exact state that he was in and saw that his eyes appeared eerily empty. All of a sudden, Jimmy started shouting at me to stop trying to kill him. I attempted to calm him down by reassuring that all was OK, but he proceeded to yell louder and louder, waking the inmates in the adjacent cells. While young Jimmy was shouting, it became apparent that he thought he was on fire, thus escalating his distress even more.

Every jail cell in NSW has a panic button, otherwise known as the knock-up button. For me to get to this button, I needed to get closer to Jimmy, which I was reluctant to do given his manic state. When Jimmy turned to face me next, I was surprised to see that he was holding a pen. I managed to momentarily distract him and he moved towards the rear window of our cell. The boys in the adjoining cells were now awake and shouting at Jimmy with concern, asking him to sit down, relax and to let me make him a cup of tea. What they couldn't see, however, was that even though Jimmy had started quietening down, his physical gestures were becoming more agitated and violent. Luckily, he became somewhat distracted near the rear window bars and I seized the opportunity to make my way to the knock-up intercom to alert the guards. Before I could press it, however, I saw that one of the few caring and friendly female officers who must have been doing her rounds and upon hearing the commotion had come to our cell. But as a sole female on patrol, she was not permitted to open the cell to potential violence.

Officer Dianne attempted to calm Jimmy down through the cell door, while I tried to explain the situation. She cautioned that there would be consequences should we need further intervention, which I knew to be in the form of extraction by the 'ninja turtles', the nickname for the special riot officers, who enter the cell in full S.W.A.T gear in response to the knock-up button. I told Officer Dianne that I saw no choice regardless. In the end, I didn't end up pressing the knock-up button as she activated the extraction procedure herself.

In anticipation of what was to come, I quickly stripped to my underwear and got on my knees in the middle of the cell with my hands over my head. Within three minutes, four officers stormed into the cell and even though Officer Dianne yelled that I was of no danger to anyone and had done nothing wrong, I was dragged out of the cell, stripped and, with my hands behind my head, made to kneel face against the wall. I watched as Jimmy, lucky to weigh fifty kilograms to each officer's 120, was dragged kicking and screaming out of our cell and to what I later found out was the mental health ward of the jail.

Unsurprisingly, I didn't sleep for the rest of the night and I later found out that Jimmy was a chronic ice addict and was coming off a recent contraband-fuelled ice binge. Unbeknownst to me was also the fact that young Jimmy was in jail for allegedly killing his partner's ex-boyfriend with a pen while on a drug bender. Suffice to say, I was hoping to avoid another young man suffering the effects of drug withdrawal as my cellie.

Jimmy's story, however, doesn't end here. Some months later when he returned from the mental ward clean of drugs, he relapsed and after another drug binge his paranoia led him to be convinced that another inmate, who happened to be a high profile NSW rapist, was his father who had raped his mother. Despite the reality that this scenario would have meant his mother giving birth to Jimmy at the age of ten, Jimmy could not let go of his obsession or shake his addiction and was very quickly returned to the mental health facility and never heard of again.

The Boneyard

In most jails, the population is broken up into two distinct areas. There is the main or general section which makes up ninety per cent of the inmates and then there is protective custody, colloquially referred to as the boneyard. The boneyard houses inmates who have given evidence against other prisoners and include former police officers, lawyers, gang members, drug dealers, white-collar criminals, inmates on the run from jail debt and of course violent and sex offenders, including child sex offenders. The more serious offenders will likely have served much of their sentence in protective custody at maximum-security jails, but could end up in a lower security prison when nearing the end of their jail time.

The term boneyard stems from the fact that the general population call fellow inmates who 'roll' – in other words, give evidence on others – a dog and dogs live in the boneyard. The canine reference, however, does not end there. That's because if you do anything wrong in protective custody and are placed in isolation (solitary confinement), you are placed in the pound.

When I was sentenced, it was determined that, due to the nature of my crime and the picture painted by the media, I would likely be subjected to attempted extortion and as such protective custody would be where I would have to serve my four years. My fellow offenders over the next few years, therefore, were those who were in danger from other inmates. However, even within this eclectic group, all things were not deemed equal and safety was most certainly not assured to all. The population formed its own justice system according to the category of crime of their fellow inmates. Child sex offenders, for example, were the bottom of the totem pole in jail and occasionally had a special punishment reserved for them as a welcome to the facility. The punishment consisted of boiling hot seeded jam until it was bubbling and throwing it in the face of the child sex offenders so that when the burns and scarring eventually healed, the seeds from the jam would still be stuck in their skin. And from that point onward, they would be easily identifiable at any jail they moved through. The senior inmates would generally task a young inmate with doling out this type of punishment. In return, they would receive rewards in the form of prescription medication or tobacco for example.

Also housed in protective custody were many high-profile offenders including former soldiers, as well as NSW northern and southern area rapists.

The Librarian

The first of a number of lessons that my mentor in jail, Gerry, let me in on was that on the inside, one needs to choose between being someone who 'loves' jail life and therefore is involved in all things gambling, drugs, fights, factions and prison politics, or alternatively, one could choose to embark on a path to self-improvement and growth. Gerry suggested that I check out the library and tell him what I thought.

Upon visiting the jail library, I couldn't believe how clean, carpeted and comfortable it was. Full of books in great condition and, despite it being a particularly hot summer's day, it was pleasant and air-conditioned. To my amazement, however, apart from a civilian librarian on duty, no one was in the library at all. Even though this seemed to be the most comfortable environment in the jail, cool in summer and warm in winter, it was clearly not very popular with the inmates.

When I reported back to Gerry about what I saw, he confirmed that that's exactly what he was hoping for. He told me that the civilian librarian was looking for an inmate library assistant and suggested that I try to get the job. The added bonus was that my jail income would be increased from $18 to the maximum of $33 per week that one was allowed to earn.

Of course, the civilian librarian was more than happy to have a literate inmate working with her and I will never forget her first bit of advice. "Make sure you check the bible shelf every day, because the boys will come in and rip the pages out to use as tally-ho paper for their tobacco."

I started working the very next day after my visit and from that point on, until the day I left, I made sure that I read a book each week.

As the librarian, my life very quickly became a routine of library work, gym, walk, sleep and repeat. Being an inmate librarian and with officers acutely aware of my past, I became very useful when they were looking for help with their personal tax returns. Unsurprisingly, it often felt like I was living in a movie. And the irony of serving time for a financial crime yet consistently turned to for financial guidance did not escape me.

The reality of being an inmate with literacy and numeracy skills meant that I suddenly discovered my survival tool on the inside. My position in the library meant that other inmates too would now come to me for help with their own legal and financial matters, particularly given the very low levels of literacy and numeracy skills amongst the prison population. Not long after starting to work in the library, I was asked if I had any interest in undertaking a TAFE course to become a librarian. Before I could even respond, my civilian librarian supervisor offered for Corrective Services to pay for the course and naturally I jumped at the chance. As I had ample time on my hands, I completed the CertIII in about six months.

About one year into my librarian life, I was unexpectedly called to the governor's or jail warden's office. I was highly anxious of course and had no idea what to expect. She sat me down and, to my great surprise, told me that I had been doing a stellar job in the library and offered me a position to work in the library at the Brushfarm Academy, the prison officer's training academy. She proceeded to explain that working there meant that each day, six other inmates and I, wearing prison greens, would go in an unmarked van to Sydney's Eastwood, where the academy was located. We would be leaving at seven a.m. for the fifteen-minute drive from Silverwater and returning at three p.m. I would be working in the library, whereas the others would be there for general garden maintenance.

Leaving jail every day was not only an incredibly welcome change of scenery, but it also meant that I would have the opportunity to converse with civilians as the facility catered to a wide range of educational and administrative programs. Brushfarm had about half a dozen civilian staff and on any given day at least 100 officers from around the state would come for the various training courses. I was allowed to eat one meal a day in the officers' dining room, where I had plenty of opportunity for social interaction.

Working at the Brushfarm library meant that I was experiencing the opposite ends of jail life at the same time.

On the one hand, I was selecting, covering, labelling and distributing books for inmates at the thirty-two correctional centres across NSW, and on the other, I was assisting officers within their own library to find reference books for their studies. I often saw the conflicted look within officers' eyes, knowing that they needed daily assistance from me, an inmate. Ironically, it would mean having to locate a crime book that was often about an inmate back in the jail that I was housed in.

The kitchen at Brushfarm was short staffed for an upcoming evening function one day. Along with two other trusted inmates, the gardeners, I was asked if we were interested in doing a night shift and wash dishes at an important graduation dinner, attended by the Minister for Corrective Services and other dignitaries. Surely enough, as we were clearing the tables, my fellow colleagues were very committed to not wanting to let anything go to waste and consumed as much of the unwanted alcohol left in the glasses as possible. It is fair to say that by the time we returned to the jail, they not only stank of alcohol, but could barely walk. Being caught in such state would mean a minimum twelve-month moratorium on external leave programs as well as causing embarrassment for the supervising officers. Luck, however, was on the inmates' side that night as I was the only one who was breath-tested upon return to jail. And those who know me would certainly see the humour in this as I have never been a fan of a drink. I am sure my colleagues, however, slept very soundly that night.

During my lunch break at Brushfarm Academy, I was permitted to sit in the courtyard to enjoy the fresh air and read my book. And that's exactly what I was doing one sunny day when six large four-wheel drive vehicles suddenly pulled up in a circle around me. A state of absolute terror engulfed me and the urge to run as fast as I could was simply overwhelming. Each of the vehicles had Public Order Riot Squad Police written on them, PORS for short. Next, about twenty heavily armed officers jumped out of the vehicles in full tactical gear. As my jail paranoia kicked in, my mind was in frantic overdrive as to what on earth I could have done to attract such attention. To my embarrassment, however, they were not interested in me at all and were purely there on a training exercise. Nonetheless, upon seeing the fear in my eyes, most pulled out their weapons and took fake aim, further capitalising on my fear. It was only when they proceeded to laugh and pull out their sand mannequins to start training, that I realised that they just could not pass up the opportunity of a prank.

The Bank Robber and the Boxer

Day three into my first of two stays at the underground hellhole of the Surry Hills Correctional Services Cells, a seemingly sympathetic officer told me that the cells were largely full and given that I was in a larger cell (five by five metres with a concrete bench that doubled as a bed along one wall) asked if I would mind sharing with someone who had just come in on similar charges to mine.

At that point, I had no idea how long I would have to be there as I was waiting for bail to be met. I was considered an NA or non-association inmate, the strictest form of protective custody, and it was deemed dangerous for me to mix with other prisoners. As such, to share the cell with anyone meant having my classification changed to LA, which stands for limited association classification and is given to inmates who are supposedly on remand for similar charges. I agreed to cooperate as I was craving company.

About an hour later, my new cell mate arrived and introduced himself as Lincoln. As I observed the man standing in my cell, it was pretty evident that I had been blindsided. Not only was Lincoln's entire mouth filled with gold teeth but he was covered in what was quite obviously long-standing jail ink. Feeling a little thrown and confused,

I broke jail etiquette and asked him what he was in for. To my astonishment, he told me that he was an armed bank robber and then the penny dropped. The officers had namely likened my financial crime as that of someone physically stealing money.

As it turned out, this was Lincoln's fourth visit to jail and despite only being in his forties, he had already spent at least fifteen years in and out of the system. I learnt that he was actually an infamous break and enter mastermind of the nineties, known as the 'hole in the wall bandit'. Apparently, according to Lincoln, his most famous escapade was cutting a hole in the roof of the colourful nightclub Blackmarket in Sydney, waiting until the club was empty and then breaking into the safe. However, as he described it, his plan was foiled when he fell through the roof and injured himself, much to the amusement of the arresting officers.

Lincoln turned out to be quite a kind soul and, possibly due to his jail experiences, the cleanest person I had ever met. Every morning and every afternoon, he would request a mop, bucket and chemicals and would scrub our cell clean. He was so paranoid about the transmission of hepatitis, the most transmitted disease in NSW jails, that he not only scrubbed the cell twice daily, but he also showered at least three times each day. And given that he was a familiar repeat offender, the general rule of breaking the 'new arrival' down did not apply. So, within reason, he got what he asked for, which of course would not have happened for a newbie like me.

Lincoln's peculiar jail routines were my first introduction to a form of institutionalisation where habits are created as a safety net or security blanket and, over time, became so ingrained that they are very difficult to break. Over the course of my four years in jail, I came across Lincoln a few times as he travelled through the NSW jail system. My final chat with him was when he told me that the authorities had just found out that he was on the run from a Queensland crime and was therefore being extradited to a Queensland jail. As it happened, while on the run from the Queensland police, he had committed an armed robbery in NSW to help his family, as it was the only life he knew. He wore his crime with a proud smile and you couldn't help but notice the ever present us vs them, or blue vs green culture.

During my first month at Silverwater, I was introduced to a well-endowed inmate called Margot. Margot was transitioning to and living as a woman, but still at the point of identifying as a man. Margot spent her days in the yard playing the guitar and serenading some of the younger and more naïve boys, always ensuring that her brightly coloured female underwear was on display outside her cell. Despite her femininity, Margot had very broad shoulders and muscular arms and so it was no surprise to find out that the previously known Ken was a former amateur boxer, but also a convicted double murderer.

Every Tuesday when the rest of the boys received their weekly grocery and toiletry buy ups, Margot's purchases, food aside, would consist of make-up, nail polish and an assortment of hair products. She had the fortune of the thickest and longest head of hair in the jail and was also known to have an extensive network of pen pals, largely made up of both male and female inmates across the NSW jails. At this stage, she had served twenty years for her crimes and had only started to transition in the final two to three years of her sentence. During her time in custody and as a former amateur boxer, Margot was in many fights and was well known to be a fierce opponent. Therefore, during her transitioning, no one dared to challenge her or provide any commentary of course. Upon her release, Margot left the jail system and reunited with her long-time female partner, who had waited for her for many years.

Haircuts and Captain America

Every jail has an inmate barber, which is a paid job earning about $25 per week. Each morning, the barber is given a comb, professional cutting scissors, electric clippers and a large supply of non-alcoholic disinfectant, all of which must be returned at the end of every day. Our jail barber, Jack, was another high-profile sex offender from the same suburbs that I had been living in before my sentencing. Each week, I would have to approach Jack, without any outward judgement, and request my weekly hair clip. Jack was a very socially engaging man and so it was no surprise how easily such a well-spoken man was able to target and charm his victims. And as the fire chief, a highly respected member of the community, he was also deemed trustworthy of course.

Another rule that one tries to abide by in jail is that, for the most part, one should try to avoid judgement, regardless of the fellow inmate's crime. While it's unavoidable to be outraged by the nature of some of the crimes, one had no choice but to try to separate a man from their wrongdoing in order to exist day to day. However, as sex offenders sit well and truly at the bottom of the jail pecking order, they were generally an unrestricted target. And as a father of three, including two daughters, I chose to not engage with Jack, but merely thanked him for his services at the end of each haircut. The reality was that I felt extremely uncomfortable and compromised each time he clipped my hair and would return to my cell feeling disturbed and unclean.

Jack was pretty much shunned by everyone and, for most of his almost eighteen years inside, would have received very little regard or proactive interaction from inmates. Given that Silverwater also serves as a transitional centre for long-term inmates re-entering the community, Jack was released six months after me in early 2015. Based on his unwaveringly engaging and self-assured disposition, even more obvious towards the end of his sentence, many inmates were convinced that this growing bravado would ultimately see him reoffend.

On the other side of the inmate pecking order was a well-known Australian army captain who we affectionately called Captain America. Every morning following muster, he proceeded to run 100 laps of the jail yard to maintain his fitness. Captain America was a former ammunitions disposal officer, tasked with the removal and destruction of ammunition no longer in use. Unfortunately, his path crossed with a number of underworld figures who persuaded him to obtain ammunition for planned terrorist activities. When the army discovered that they could not account for ten missing rocket launchers, he was arrested and charged. Several of the rocket launchers were traced into the hands of known underworld figures and, to this day, at least five remain missing and unaccounted for.

Despite this transgression, Captain America was very proud of his service and unlike those in jail whose crimes were of a violent or sexual nature, Captain America was well liked and respected. His ultimate shame took place the day the Australian Defence Force arrived and all inmates, apart from Captain America were locked in their cell while a formal dishonourable discharge ceremony took place in the jail yard. This public humiliation was the final indignity for betraying his country and I suspect that it would have hit Captain America harder than his jail sentence. He was released nine months after me and to this day maintains a very low profile.

I am not really sure where a Jewish white-collar offender sat in the jail's pecking order, but as long as I had no trouble, I didn't really care. I stayed clear of most people and immersed myself in books, exercise and listening to my transistor radio. The radio was jail-issued and available on the monthly buy-up. I clipped it to my belt, always wore headphones and had it with me most of the time. The only problem was that it was battery-operated and new batteries were expensive and would mean forgoing other shopping items from the grocery buy-up when they needed replacement.

Regardless of the diverse, colourful and often scary backgrounds of the inmates, the playing field was pretty even on the inside.

An officer once told me, "Remember, Simon, to everyone here in green, you are just a glorified and intelligent thief."

Mobile Phones and Contraband

One of the most serious offences an inmate can commit in jail is to be found in possession of a mobile phone. And to my knowledge, a mobile phone and charger could only be smuggled into the jail in two ways. The first is via an internal cavity, charger and all, and the other is through financially incentivising a prison officer.

My first encounter with a mobile phone was while working out in the gym, which was essentially an outdoor workout area. I noticed two young inmates acting quite suspiciously near the leg-raise bar. Before I could even figure out what they were up to, about a dozen officers surrounded the gym. Apparently, they had received intel that the young boys had a mobile phone. It turned out that the mobile phone was not smuggled in for communicating with the outside, but purely for watching online porn. But in a jail with a high percentage of sex offenders, this was an especially serious offence and both boys were sent straight to the pound, the punishment cell within the boneyard. After two weeks there, both were shipped off to a remote country working jail.

My second and more intimate encounter with a mobile phone was one night while locked in my cell with my first roommate. There was a huge commotion in the cell next door that housed the brother of an Olympic medallist. He shared his cell with a well-known Asian drug mule. Unbeknownst to my cellie and me, they had been in possession of a mobile phone. Lucky for them, however, they had been tipped off and knew that officers would be raiding their cell that night and therefore had disposed of the mobile. The raiding officers had no idea about the tip-off and, upon not finding anything in the cell, followed protocol and extended their search for the mobile phone to the cells on either side. Consequently, my cellie and I were also stripped naked, dragged into the common area and thoroughly searched to ensure that we weren't complicit in hiding the mobile. After hours of searching, the phone was never located and I later found out that it was hidden in the laundry the whole time. Despite trying to stay out of trouble, being in the wrong place at the wrong time was bound to happen from time to time and often with unpleasant consequences.

The drug mule and the brother of the Olympian were also renowned for their excellence in brewing jail alcohol, otherwise known as firewater. It was generally concocted out of a combination of flowers, vegetables, smuggled yeast and cleaning chemicals. It was made in large twenty-litre garbage bags and could do some serious damage to the lining of the consumer's gut.

On my first Christmas in jail, our wing was permitted to have a Christmas lunch. We set up tables and chairs, pooled our grocery buy-ups for the week and the jail supplied Christmas Day turkey slices. Our resident brewers got to work and offered everyone a glass of firewater. I took one sip and all I tasted was metal, but even worse was the lightning bolt sensation similar to swallowing a tablespoon of wasabi. Needless to say, it was the first and last time that I dared to drink the brew and avoided being offered any again. Even as a non-drinker, it would be unpopular to reject a drink by another inmate, especially on Christmas Day.

On my last Christmas Day in jail, about five weeks before my release, I heard a large bang on the grass in front of my wing. A few of us went out to see what had happened and to our amazement noticed that a drone, which was a relatively new toy in 2014, had been flown into the jail and landed outside. Not only did the drone have drugs on board, but also had the names of the recipient and the sender written on it. When the officers and inmates saw the drone and the clear labelling, everyone roared with laughter. Then, to add to the entertainment value, the drone was flown and landed into the wrong jail yard. Needless to say, the guards had an easy time tracking down both the pilot and intended recipient. For the rest of us, however, this was a rare moment when everyone was united in amusement.

Other creative ways of landing contraband into the jail yard included filling tennis balls with drugs, papier-mâché rocks and, most bizarrely, dead birds. All these were thrown or catapulted over the twelve-metre double barbed wire fence, mostly in the middle of the night. Items were generally not addressed to the receiver. However, jail etiquette ensured that the rightful owner had first dibs. You simply didn't touch what was not intended to be yours.

The Sweeper

Before working as a librarian, I spent my first couple of weeks at Silverwater employed as the office sweeper. Each morning and afternoon, I would go into the lookout compound overlooking the yard and clean the officers' kitchen, mop the floors, empty the bins and wipe all desks. This trusted job enabled me to listen to officers' gossip and find out about their not so subtle plans for searching, otherwise known as ramping, certain inmates' cells for contraband. I made sure to not breach this trust and pass on any information to inmates to avoid being labelled a snitch for either party. Most days, the officers in the compound would ask me if I knew what certain inmates were up to, but my answer was always the same in saying, 'I'm new here and keep to myself.'

Owning and wearing high-end sneakers provides a highly sought-after standing in jail. Essentially, unless an inmate had a doctor's certificate and their family sent expensive shoes under the guise of orthopaedic assistance, everyone had to wear 'boob shoes', as was their slang term. Boob shoes are either Velcro green Dunlop KT 26 or the world's most uncomfortable Velcro Dunlop Volleys. Those lucky enough to have come from country or remote jails were allowed to bring branded high-end sneakers because the practicality of being in a remote jail necessitated better shoes. Others in possession of good shoes were also those on works release. In any case, high-end sneakers were a currency within the jail system. Many boys were often stood over or beaten for their shoes.

My responsibilities as a sweeper included being tasked to clean a room that held all the confiscated items in the jail, which included items such as lighters, shoes, boxing gloves, smuggled protein powder and tobacco. As I was heading towards the storage room to clean it one day, my protector, Kovaks, caught up with me and subtly reminded me of our first encounter when I arrived in jail. He then proceeded to tell me that he would like to have a particular pair of Nike shoes that he knew to be in the storage room. To deny his request did not even cross my mind as an option at the time.

Once inside the room, I quickly found the shoes Kovaks wanted and, in what was my only official jail misdemeanour, I also found a pair of shoes for myself. After all, who can resist a pair of Kayanos? I quickly put both pairs of sneakers in a black garbage bag and next realised that I did not have a plan to get them out of the storeroom. But as luck would have it, a very helpful inmate called Nick was in charge of emptying all the large garbage bins that day. A seasoned inmate, he had done twenty years and was quick to catch on to my mission and assisted me by leaving a large garbage bin outside the storeroom door. At the top of his voice, he then reminded me to empty all the garbage into the bin. I quickly obliged and threw the garbage bags with the two pairs of shoes into the bin. By the time I had finished cleaning the storage room, Nick had moved the rubbish bin, and the garbage bag with the shoes had mysteriously found their way to Kovaks's room.

Soon after, Kovaks gave me my shoes but the euphoria of comfortable shoes lasted about four hours. A jealous inmate snitched on me and, before long, I was being questioned by officers trying to establish how many pairs of shoes I had removed from storage. I owned up only to the pair I was wearing, which was immediately confiscated, and I lost my trusted job on the spot. Remarkably, I was not charged with any formal jail offence as that would have stayed on my jail record. The only upside to this mission was that all the other inmates knew that I stayed 'staunch' and did not give up Kovaks or Nick who had assisted. This was, in fact, my first jail stripe, which in this instance referred to not snitching on my fellow inmates. On the other hand, thinking that walking the yard in branded shoes would not draw unwanted attention was an embarrassingly rookie error of judgement on my part.

Justice Health

Justice Health provides health care to people within the correctional system and encompasses general practitioners, dentistry, optometry and mental health services. One of my first experiences with Justice Health was early in my sentence as I walked into the yard and saw a long line of jittery-looking inmates lining up at a window. Almost like a cafeteria, inmates were waiting to be served their daily meds, prompted to get in line by the PA system call of 'Pills'. Pills are handed out quite generously in jail, probably because it is a safer option for officers to have a calm and subdued population. It took little time to learn a whole new lexicon of medications and their slang terms. Seroquel, Avanza, all the Oxy family of medications were in high demand and another very valuable pill was Gabapentin, affectionately known as Gabas.

Inmates would often and openly trade pills between each other depending on what 'trips' they were trying to achieve through their home-made cocktails. Sadly, the downside is that given that all medication is dispensed for free and easily, many inmates who enter the jail system with no reliance on prescription medication can end up with an addiction on the inside. It was confronting to see so many of them high,

I suspect to numb the impact of jail. Unfortunately, when they eventually leave jail with an addiction and can't afford their habit, they are at risk of offending again and therefore continuing their cycle of crime.

The wait to see a doctor, dentist or optometrist could often be up to twelve months, unless the officers or registered nurse feel that a life was in danger. A doctor was scheduled to come to my jail once a week for an hour but, more often than not, only appeared fortnightly.

My personal experience with Justice Health was across three separate incidents. The first occasion was when I was coming off the anti-anxiety medication, Zoloft, which I had been taking during the stresses of the trial. Protocol simply required that I be examined, which I would say was half-hearted at best.

Jail became a much bigger sensory overload as soon as the medication wore off. My general awareness was heightened and I was acutely aware of the possibility of confrontational situations. It is true that surviving jail requires almost a sixth sense in anticipation about what could happen through even the slightest movement or sound. In the yard, for example, the ever moving dynamic of different gangs and groups meant that the potential for mass violence was always simmering. To even in be in the close proximity of a fight, even when not involved, would have punishable consequences. Jail punishment from officers could be loss of phone privileges, loss of grocery buy-up, suspended visits or a week in the pound.

To this day, more than six years after my release, I remain eagle-eyed in most situations. When I sit in a room, I generally have to make sure that I face or at least am aware of all entry and exit points. It is also very difficult for me to sit with my back to human movement or entrances. I am also still triggered by the sound of rattling keys. As we were locked in our cells, the officers would swing their keys most nights as if taunting to indicate that they were about to open the cell doors. Doing so would either mean being put on a truck to another jail with no warning, also known as an escort, or could indicate a cell search, or even a complete raid of the wing which would result in everyone being cuffed and stripped.

My second encounter with Justice Health was when I was inadvertently caught in the middle of a fight in the kitchen of my wing, about six months after I arrived. Two inmates started trading blows over the use of the stainless-steel percolator as they were both desperate for a coffee. The mundaneness of jail cannot hide the trigger within violent men. As I came around the corner to the kitchen, the two fighting men knocked a kettle of boiling water towards me spilling all the hot water on my bare feet. I was wearing thongs and, within seconds, the skin on the top of one foot was bubbling and blistering. I screamed in agony but had to focus on ducking the fight and avoiding further harm as one of the men proceeded to grab the sandwich maker to beat the other. In jail, this is known as getting 'Brevilled'. Thankfully, someone called for an officer to come and assist. The officer, upon seeing the state of my burn, rushed me to the nurse for attention. My foot was bandaged and took about a month to heal.

My third encounter was not as dangerous as it was humiliating. I had slipped over and rolled my ankle and knee in the gym. The pain in my knee was so intense that I couldn't sleep. It was only when I told the nurse and the supervising officer that my injury was a result of me being in the gym that their duty of care instincts kicked in. They arranged for me to go on an escorted trip to Westmead hospital for scans. Two officers cuffed me and put me in a secure vehicle for the fifteen-minute drive to the hospital. Both officers warned me that I would feel very uncomfortable once we entered the hospital but I did not think much of what they had said. As soon as we got out of the vehicle, however, one of the officers told me that he was going to place my sweater over my cuffed hands, not just to save me any embarrassment in public, but also to avoid frightening women or children. That narrative hit me like a tonne of bricks. The thought that someone would consider me scary and dangerous simply gutted and froze me. Sure enough, as I was escorted down the hallway, cuffs covered but dressed in prison green, I could see the fear in people's eyes as they looked at me.

Suffice to say, this was definitely one of the lowest points of my jail life. I can't even recall speaking to the doctor because all I remember is the overwhelming realisation of the low point at which I now was.

C3, With Leave

Jail is all about setting goals to make your time pass. The jail system is structured around performance hurdles and a classification process that can ultimately lead the inmate to the highest reward of work release. To achieve the goal, inmates must work their way through the A, B and C levels of classification, the goal being to secure that of C3, with leave. Only about 150 out of 13,000 inmates achieve the classification each year.

After almost a year at the jail library and a further two at the Brushfarm Academy, I earned the right to become a C3 classified inmate, the lowest security classification within the NSW jail system. C3 with leave enabled an inmate to get a job and once a month be granted day or weekend leave to spend with an approved sponsor. The approved sponsor is heavily vetted by the jail system to ensure that they are an upstanding member of society.

To this day, I find it hard to find the words of gratitude towards two incredible friends, willing to give up their weekends so that I could stay with them once a month during my final year in jail. The weekends were especially important as they also enabled me to see my three children. And as leave privileges included the ability to spend a few hours at the closest shopping centre from the sponsor's home, my children were able to sit with me in a Westfield food court and we had the chance to connect on the outside and, for a few hours, be a family.

Some of the realities of the leave program meant that I had to wear an ankle monitor. The monitor back then was not small and when wearing shorts, could only be hidden by bandaging the ankle. I chose to hide my anklet by always wearing long pants. There is a stigma attached to monitoring anklets in that they are perceived as being worn mainly by sex offenders. Then there are the young men who as repeat offenders knew the system and proudly wore their anklet in public as a badge of honour. Hence it was often colloquially called a Rooty Hill Rolex. Those who were proud to show their 'jewellery' were usually the boys who also proudly displayed their postcode in large font tattooed on their neck.

As a result of staff shortages and the length of time to arrange each leave weekend, I managed to secure about nine weekend excursions. On almost every occasion that I was on leave, plain-clothes officers would either visit my sponsor's house unannounced for a random breath test for drugs and alcohol, which were of course forbidden, or they would hide in the shopping centre where I was catching up with my family to ensure that I wasn't meeting with other criminals.

The works release part of my leave program saw me starting work at Our Big Kitchen (OBK), a community kitchen in Bondi. While for most people, the thought of hours every day on public transport would be draining, for me it was one of the most exciting parts of the day. Every day, I spent two hours in the morning catching a bus and two trains from Silverwater to Bondi and at the end of the day, two hours on the return trip. Private transport, cars, taxis, were forbidden and only public transport was allowed. As I travelled both trips at peak hour daily, the buses and trains were always full. I did not have a mobile phone or laptop, as they were also not allowed. Work release inmates also had to catch specific buses and trains at certain times each day and no deviation from the most direct route to and from work was permitted. Therefore, if a food store happened to be in between transport routes, we were able to stop and purchase something, but were not allowed to sit and dine or stray in any way from the approved route.

I was on a public bus with two other inmates one day somewhere between Strathfield station and Silverwater when it broke down. In any circumstance of a delay, it was incumbent on us to advise the jail that we would be late and past our designated curfew. For me, the stress of never missing a bus, train or being late back to jail was sometimes overwhelming. And so I immediately took it upon myself to ask a member of the general public if I could borrow his phone. The absurdity of asking a stranger for their phone to call my jail did not escape me and I thought the guy would be scared at my request. To my surprise, however, his response was, "No worries, cuz, my bro is inside anyway."

He proceeded to enquire whether his brother was known to me or the other boys, which he was not. I can't remember the good Samaritan's name, but he also kindly offered to show us some adult entertainment and order pizza while we waited for the replacement bus. After calling the jail, and reporting the incident including the bus, registration and the driver's details for verification, we waited an hour for the replacement bus. Sadly, there was no opportunity for pizza, but plenty of idle time for watching porn.

Work Release For a Living

The work release program is designed to reinstate inmates who have served medium to long-term sentences back into society. Work release enables inmates to have an approved job at an approved location. The vetting process to authorise a business for work release is extensive and, generally speaking, the jobs are in the blue-collar sector.

The anticipated result of work release is for an inmate to leave jail with new skills and ongoing employment to support himself and dependants. The immediate financial reality of this program while on the inside however was that twenty per cent of the income had to be paid to the jail for rent, an additional $60 per week was then charged for the ankle-monitoring bracelet while out in public and a further $60 each week was spent on transport by way of an opal card. In my case, after these expenses, I was able to send $200 a week to my family, leaving me with $100 for my weekly food and phone calls.

The first day that I was able to once again dress in civilian clothing and go to work was a complete high. Ditching the 24/7 jail greens felt like stepping out of my skin. I had a new shirt, pants and shoes, ready for my first day at a new job. Nervously, I walked out of the jail with a strange sensation, albeit true that my every move was being watched. I got on the bus outside the jail to Auburn station and then I caught a train to Sydney's shopping and transport hub, Bondi Junction, my old neighbourhood and comfort zone over many years. That now seems so very long ago.

As soon as I got off the train at Bondi Junction, I was absolutely overcome by fear. Having to walk past Westfield Bondi Junction and almost touching the life I once lived, not to mention the prospect of bumping into former friends and colleagues, was totally petrifying. And so I remember my first trip to work quite clearly. I walked with my head down and as fast as I could towards OBK, also known as the Kitchen, the community kitchen in Flood Street, Bondi, about fifteen minutes from the station.

My very first task at my new job was to mop the floors and clean the toilet. To my surprise, even doing something so mundane completely lifted my spirits.

When I finished my first job, my friend Gerry, who had left the jail two years earlier and was now the GM of OBK, said to me, "Simon, in this kitchen, we make food for those who are homeless, victims of domestic violence, refugees and those who are completely forgotten in the community. I asked you to clean the toilet and mop the floors, because I guarantee you that those who we make food for wish that they had a clean and safe toilet to use."

Every day at the Kitchen was a new experience. Over the two years that I was there, I learnt to make a vast range of meals in bulk quantities and I'd like to think that I mastered the art of baking cakes, pies, breads and biscuits. I believe that to this day, some of my recipes are still being used. I also quickly learnt that making a thousand meals a day for those less fortunate presented a spiritual reward that was completely unfamiliar. There is no doubt that in my previous life, I wrote cheques for a range of charities, but I never felt the impact of my philanthropy. Being so part of the process of a charitable, not-for-profit function was a completely new and humbling experience.

Different groups of people were forever on rotation, assisting in preparing the meals at the Kitchen. Included were schoolkids, university groups and local businesses of any size, all the way to large multinational corporates. Some days there were up to 150 people on site helping to prepare meals.

Before preparing the meals, we would always set the scene with a motivational and inspirational talk. Gerry and others would tell the story behind the Kitchen, always emphasising that in life, everyone deserves a second chance and that second chances were OBK's mission. Gerry would also tell his own story of incarceration and the second chance that he was given through the Kitchen.

We were hosting a large group of banking executives as corporate volunteers one day and Gerry was not at work. I was asked to give the welcome talk in his absence and incorporate a short version of my journey to OBK. Telling my story to complete strangers and the reaction this evoked was both unexpected and powerful. And I had this moment of epiphany that, for better or worse, my story is for me to own. And from that time, I have told a version of the following many times.

> *I'm going to tell you a story about Mr X. Mr X was born into a life of luxury with a silver spoon in his mouth. The best schools, the best houses, the best of everything. However, as Mr X became a successful businessman later in life, he took his successes for granted as he always thought that he rode on the coat tail of his family and all he really had was charm and a nice smile. Mr X had a beautiful house, a wife and three children and all the trappings of a six-star life. But Mr X took some financial shortcuts in some of his business dealings that were far from kosher. One day, there was a knock at Mr X's door. It was the police telling Mr X that he was under arrest for his financial improprieties. Mr X was taken to a police station and charged with 227 counts of fraud, totalling over $16 million. During the process, Mr X would find himself before the judge, who said, 'Mr X, despite your standing in the community and good work you have done, I am sentencing you to six and a half years in jail, of which you must serve a minimum of four years.' Fast forward, Mr X was walking the jail yard and around him saw men who were in jail as a result of their actions, and often stuck in a generational cycle of drugs, alcohol and sexual abuse. It was at this point that Mr X, ironically, recognised how lucky he was. Despite being in jail, he was*

clothed, housed and fed. This humbling realisation carried Mr X through his jail sentence to never judge anybody for their actions. And where is Mr X today? Mr X stands before you. I am Mr X.

Every time I told this story to an audience, the gradual realisation that Mr X was in many ways somebody just like them was quite obvious. I would generally finish my story by talking about the pitfalls of shortcuts, avoiding judgement and I've come to learn first-hand that everybody deserves a second chance. Without fail, there was always an instant bond with the group I spoke to. I always left time for questions at the end and they were generally the same four. 1) What was the food like? 2) Are there conjugal visits? 3) Did you get in any fights? 4) Did your children visit you?

A large group of property executives from a well-known listed property fund came to the Kitchen one day, many of whom I had dealt with in a previous life. When I told them my story, many already knew the ending. When the session was over, most of the twenty-five men and women came over for a hug or to shake my hand and, to this day, I remain in touch with many.

As one would expect, thoughts about where my life would be today, had I chosen a different path, have not been far from my mind, especially in the early years. Telling the story about Mr X, which I have done many times, was always a sure way to bring back the crushing guilt and the 'what if' wonderings.

Attila My Mum

One of the most uplifting times to work at the Kitchen was during school holidays. Every day of the holidays, we ran OOSH (Out of School Hours) programs for anywhere between forty and 120 children. The cultural diversity of the children was what made the programs so rewarding. Each program was run like a military operation. There was always cookie and bread making and we also included callisthenics. Children would be divided into three groups and we would make sure that kids of different backgrounds were matched with the purpose of taking them a little out of their comfort zone, because even at such a young age it was important to encourage an inclusive, no judgement mentality.

Hosting other not for profit organisations in the Kitchen was common. One such was known as Together For Humanity (TFH) and is an interfaith charity that brings together students of Jewish, Islamic and Christian faith-based schools. TFH teaches kids how to celebrate each other's faith and background through learning about individuals' beliefs and culture. The end of the program involved bonding over the one thing they all had in common, food. This part required each group of kids preparing meals unique to their own faith and ethnicity. The result was sharing recipes, collaboration and connection. What I would always notice among these children of assorted beliefs was the camaraderie that we all in Australia have in laughing and joking about sport and music. The old saying, 'Let's break bread', never held more truth to me than when each culture would prepare their version of bread to share with the other.

As we did with our corporate programs, we conducted a welcome to the Kitchen session to set the scene with the other guests too. Obviously, telling my jail story was not age-appropriate and so I chose to tell another second chance story when I was asked to present. In such cases, I chose to tell the story about how my family came to Australia as refugees in the 1940s. It gave me the chance to show the opportunities that Australia had given to those from other countries. My story to our young visitors was always told in the third person.

> *There was a young couple that met eighty years ago in Poland and fell in love. What should have been the happiest time in their lives unfortunately turned out to be the opposite. The Nazi regime was sweeping across the region and sadly, as this young couple saw their brothers, sisters and family killed in concentration camps and the war, they had no choice but to fight for their own survival. They managed to smuggle themselves out of Poland and after a six-month journey, they arrived in a country that was then known as the British Mandate of Palestine.*

Over the next few years, they worked hard in a country that was very under-developed and lacking in basic living standards. The husband worked for the British government and the wife stayed home as they had a baby. When the baby girl turned three, Palestine was on the brink of a civil war and the year was 1946 and the world was trying to figure out how to help the struggling nation.

Fearing for their lives and not wanting to raise their daughter in a potential war zone, they once again escaped and spent the next nine months at sea travelling to a new home. During that time, they were stuck in port for three months in Bombay when the young girl, who by now was three, developed a scoliosis. And as a result and even as an adult, she did not grow beyond four feet eleven. The poor girl also developed chronic hair lice and, because there were no quick treatments in those days like today, her entire head was shaved to get rid of the lice. Despite the challenging journey, the young family finally arrived in Launceston, Tasmania.

It was 1947 now and at that time, the people in Tasmania had not encountered a young Jewish family with names that they could not pronounce. The young family's names were Uri, Dora and Batia Eisenstadt. However, the family was welcomed with open arms and without judgement. They rented a small apartment above a shop and while the little girl started school, Uri and Dora would mend stockings for a living.

After a few years of hard work, they also rented the shop below and had a thriving tailor business. Uri was so proud of the country that had taken them in that he decided that he wanted to change their names to sound more Australian. He went to the local registry office and asked the man what the most Australian names that he had. The man told Uri that the most Aussie name that he could have was Ken and that Dora was already a pretty popular name and she should keep it. And Batia had her name changed to Betty. Ken decided that Eisenstadt was also a bit difficult and as it translated from German to English to mean steel city, they changed their last name to Steele. And they became known as Ken, Dora and Betty Steele. Many years later, young Betty had children of her own. And one of those children, her eldest son, stands here before you. I am the proud child and grandchild of a refugee and original boat person.

Telling this story to my young audience gave me great pleasure. As they mostly came from different ethnic backgrounds, I hoped that they would see a connection between my story and theirs. And they did. I relished seeing the penny drop in their little faces.

Grateful Groundhog Day

Coffee in jail was available three ways. Firstly, in small sachets handed out with breakfast, the quality and taste of which points to unusable coffee that must have been left over on a coffee factory floor. The second way was on the grocery buy-up as supermarket-style coffee sachets, and the third, for me, was when three times a year as a Jewish inmate, I would be sent jail-approved care packages for the Jewish Holidays by Jewish Care. There would always be 500 grams of high-quality ground coffee, which, although it was a highly sought-after commodity, I was never willing to trade. The other items included tinned pickles, tinned eggplant, cake, nuts, olives and other food items, which were also in great demand.

Every day of the work release program, leaving jail and returning in the evening was like a Groundhog Day of freedom, followed by lock-up and repeat. Each morning would bring the elation of getting dressed in civilian clothing, making sure my monitoring anklet was covered and embarking on the two-hour trip to the Kitchen. And each day en route, I indulged in one little pleasure that I had time for and could also afford. I would stop at a little café in Bondi Junction and savour the taste of a real barista-made double espresso. I would always order my coffee and stand about a foot back form the counter and shop entry to drink it. Any closer in could have breached the rule of dining in or taking the most direct course to work. Even today, when I am in the neighbourhood, I enjoy the occasional coffee at the same café. But now, I mostly sit down and savour the moment and sometimes the eerie feeling of possibly being watched comes over me.

The flip side of my daily routine to and from work was returning to jail, which would entail a lengthy interview about what possible contraband I was possibly looking to smuggle into jail and, more often than not, involved some kind of strip search, the length of which depended on which officer was on duty that night. There was one particular officer, universally disliked by both inmates and fellow officers. When he was on duty, he did everything possible to make the process of re-entering jail as uncomfortable and personally invasive as possible, to the point of checking any clothing features that could possibly carry contraband, including the soles of shoes for any hidden compartments and pulling out the inner sole of the shoes too. On one occasion, I had accidentally left a chapstick in my pocket on return to jail and this particular officer, as a show of authority, rolled the balm out of the case and threw the whole thing away.

The archaic way that jails in NSW are run means that all inmate administrative functions are completed longhand on paper and rarely electronically. Of course, this was a great way for officers to exercise subjectivity and take the law into their own hands by saying at their discretion that the paperwork got lost. Any movement in and out of jail for an inmate and any requests, be it new phone numbers on the call list, doctors' appointments, visitor requests and so on, were all handwritten and required three signatures from ranking officers. Every day would bring the anxiety of whether my warrant to leave had been signed, which in turn meant that every day at six a.m. an officer would fumble around looking for the necessary paperwork before I could leave. As part of this process, it also meant that I could be up, showered, dressed and ready to work, waiting for the officer on duty to unlock my cell to even start the daily release process. Every day I was anticipating the officer, fearing that I might be late to the designated routes, which would trigger a chain reaction of a new route, lateness to work, worried employer and calls between jail and work.

There were numerous instances where the paperwork had not been executed and we were not able to leave to go to work. The consequence was often that our employers were being inconvenienced and ended up calling the jail demanding that we be let out. While this tactic would generally work, the officers would inevitably end up feeling insulted and in turn made sure that we received 'special treatment' on our return to jail. Losing face or 'being put on show' as it was known, was a lose-lose situation for all.

Back at the Kitchen (OBK)

Welcoming a different group of volunteers every day opened my eyes to the business end of the not-for-profit world. The Kitchen required an ever-changing roster of volunteers to cook and serve the meals and the delicate balance of sourcing fresh supplies and securing the workforce to ensure that meals were prepared was an ongoing challenge.

The practicality of feeding the disadvantaged was also something that never occurred to me. For example, in feeding the homeless, meals have to be very soft, because the dental health of many was so poor that a hearty, chewy meal would simply be a struggle to eat, causing embarrassment and distress. On the other hand, when catering to women housed in temporary accommodation, often as the result of domestic violence, ensuring that meals were freezer-friendly and easily transportable was key, in the event that the they had to move location quickly. The Kitchen also catered to many frontline and emergency service workers, in which case meals had to be high in protein and safe to be consumed without refrigeration or defrosting.

I certainly came to understand that one of the keys to running a successful not-for-profit organisation was the ability to discover and leverage all financial incentive programs the government had to offer. In terms of jail work release programs in NSW, this included most inmates in the program having their wages subsidised by up to seventy-five per cent. In my case, despite being in a religiously run organisation, a cash payment was the best course of action to secure my employment. Without hesitation, Chaim 'greased the palm' to the tune of $5,000 so I could start work.

In addition to inmates, the Kitchen also engaged a number of overseas university students on internship programs. As their visa prohibited them to be paid, their labour was free. Furthermore, on any given day, there were between two and twenty unpaid volunteers working in the Kitchen as well. And every afternoon, up to twenty high school kids would also volunteer to accumulate their community service volunteer hours.

It is safe to say that the cost of labour at the Kitchen was negligible, other than that of senior management. And given the amount of good food in Australia that ends up in landfill, there are many food aggregators including OzHarvest, Second Bite and Food Bank, thanks to whom perishables, non-perishables and general items can be either purchased for minimal cost or in some instances donated at no cost. And therefore, when the cost of labour and goods combined are minimal, it allows for a thriving charity with all the trimmings of maximum impact and vast output for those in need.

At any given time, there were between two and five inmates working at the Kitchen. As the work involved working with women, children, vulnerable groups including those with special needs, youth at risk and juvenile justice, the general rule was to only employ inmates whose crimes were not considered of a violent or sexual nature. As the Kitchen's motto was second chances, however, it was decided to employ two violent offenders. One of them was a murderer who was known in legal circles as a vexatious litigant who denied his crime and who today is back in and out of jail as a result of extortion and impersonating a police officer.

The second inmate was a high profile double murderer, who murdered and dismembered his ex-lovers and later while on parole cut off his monitoring bracelet and went on the run.

Some other inmates working at OBK were also repeat offenders, but did not fall into either category of a dangerous or minimal risk offender. One of those in this grey area was a young man with a colourful past. On one occasion, as I went to retrieve some items from a storage cage, I caught him being orally pleasured by one of the young foreign university students participating in the internship program. After processing the scene, I quickly realised that I had two choices. One was to report it immediately, knowing that it would likely mean the end of the work release program at OBK and of course I feared that would put my employment and income in jeopardy. Alternatively, I could simply confront my work release colleague and remind him that he was not only putting himself at risk, but also everyone else's employment, which most certainly would do no favours in the jail yard for him. To my relief and surprise, he took our chat well and was quite remorseful, immediately owning his wrongdoing. To my knowledge, there were no further indiscretions.

Another OBK program for refugees was through a charity called House of Welcome, a residential refugee centre in Villawood that similarly focused on the integration of refugees into the community through food. At the time I worked at the Kitchen, we collaborated with the House of Welcome to educate visitors about the many ways that refugees landed in Australia. The event would invite guest refugee speakers from the Middle East and India who spoke of often harrowing stories in their homeland and then expressed their gratitude to Australia by preparing a traditional meal for everyone to taste. In light of my background, I always found these events highly relatable. Personally, however, they were very humbling.

Each week, the Kitchen made the request of the jail that I work late one night to assist in running and organising charitable Challah Bakes, the traditional Jewish Sabbath bread. Many of the bakes were arranged in honour of a bride getting married or a baby about to be born, but in the majority of instances, the bake was intended to either raise funds for sick members of the Jewish community or to lift the spirits of families going through a hard time. Even though OBK was operated by an orthodox Jewish rabbi, it was, in essence, a non-denominational charity supporting every group of the Australian community. For me, working at an event where someone's misfortune was through no fault of their own allowed me less room for self-pity, despite the fact that my day-to day-life was at one of its lowest points. I was where I was through my own volition. I fronted many events at the Kitchen that reinforced this perspective and I think it gave me some strength to see my sentence through and determination to start life again.

Yard Culture

As an older, ethnic inmate, I did not fit into the traditional jail yard groups. They were generally made up of the 'Koori boys', Chinese crew, Vietnamese boys, the Middle Eastern mix and the assortment of Eastern Europeans. I was certainly not seen as a traditional Australian either. But it was advisable, in some way, to connect with all the groups.

The easiest way to gain a little bit of street cred in the jail yard was to play the daily afternoon game of touch football. In those first two years, after the library closed each day, I would join the boys for a couple of hours of highly boisterous footy. Although mostly played in the spirit of the game, in view of the eclectic collection of offenders, tempers often flared. Adding to the drama of the game was the fact that the playing area was more gravel than grass. Respect was easily earned based on your skill on the football field and as one of the few unmedicated inmates, my reflexes and ball skills were better than those of many. It was during one of these matches that I realised the fine line that we all walked each day to maintain peace. The wrong word said at any time during a match could easily set off a mini race riot, making every game a minefield that could erupt at any time.

I remember when one such game degenerated into endless name calling and threats and oddly the peace only came when a couple of the older Vietnamese men, who were spectators, invited everyone for a bit of a communal cook-up. As a special treat, they added some extra protein and flavour to the cook-up, thanks to the ibis that they had earlier caught and killed with homemade dart guns, using Bic pen casings. They would corner the ibis or pigeon and when the bird was trapped, they would, with incredible accuracy, blow multiple darts, made of sewing needles, at the neck of the bird. As soon as the bird was injured, it would be captured and its neck snapped. I once unknowingly had a mouthful of pigeon, but did not taste the ibis. I am sure the officers knew exactly what was going on, but as long as the yard was peaceful, they were happy.

Interestingly, the two best chefs in the jail during my stay were highly regarded drug cooks on the outside. Their life, in whatever country they lived in, always revolved around cooking meth. In jail, these older, respected Asian men would often take some of the younger Asian boys under their wing. The boys were often in jail as a result of being drug mules, the irony being that they were most likely jailed as a result of transporting and concealing drugs that the older men had cooked. As my jail was a transitional centre, many of these foreign drug-related inmates would, especially towards the end of their sentence, be kicked out of Australia. In the middle of the night, many would be driven to the airport and quietly deported back to their homeland, whereas others would await deportation at the Villawood Detention Centre after their release from jail.

If the inmate was not an Australian citizen and facing deportation after jail, their visa would be revoked as they had failed the government's character test. I would often hear boys who knew that they would be deported plotting their fight against their deportation through all avenues, which could result in extending their stay in Australia by up to three years, albeit in the confines of a detention centre. The reality for them was that they had nothing to go home to. A detention centre, however, offered them some semblance of a life.

Jail Ingenuity

Surviving in jail sometimes required McGyver-like ingenuity. For instance, getting a tattoo is a serious offence and obviously there is no tattooing equipment. But that does not stop the boys tattooing themselves, be it through carving into their own skin and filling the cuts with a pen, or asking the Islander boys to perform traditional rock, ink and hammer methods. Another very painful, but ingenious, tattoo method in jail involved taking a desk fan, removing all the blades and wire casing and attaching a knitting needle dipped ink to the spinning motor of the fan, thereby creating an electric tattoo gun. These were generally only operated by the more skilled jail tattooists. I never quite worked out how the boys thought that officers would not notice their newly acquired ink.

Another interesting discovery was the way in which most of the drugs were brought into the jail. Of course, the majority of interaction with the outside world took place during weekend visits. The boys who had permission to wear branded sneakers would ask their visitors to wear exactly the same sneakers as them during the visit. The visitor's sneakers would hide drugs and when the guards weren't looking and as there were no cameras in the visiting area of my jail, the inmate and visitor would swap shoes. The inmate would then take the chance of being searched or detected by a sniffer dog at the end of the visit. Another ingenious method that I witnessed was disguising drugs as a tooth. When a visitor and inmate would greet or farewell with a kiss, the tooth would be slid into the latter's mouth and the drugs bought into the jail. Clearly, this plan hinged on both parties missing at least one tooth and was generally intended for self-use rather than distribution.

My personal favourite jail creativity, which I proudly participated in, was our homemade gym equipment. For safety reasons, free weights were not permitted in jail and only a limited number of gym machines were available. We would therefore collect an assortment of empty chemical bottles ranging from two-litre to twenty-litre drums and fill them with water from the bathroom and rocks from the yard and then tether them on either end of broomsticks. We quickly learnt that the heaviest weights we could create without compromising the broomsticks were bottles each weighing twenty-five kilos. We also made weight benches out of milk crates that were used for food deliveries. Occasionally, when everyone was locked in their cells, a spiteful officer would either break the broomsticks or puncture the drums, triggering the whole process of the gym's creation to start again.

Although I never saw this in action, I was told that homemade drug kits were plentiful and necessary for drugs that can only be consumed when they are inhaled off heated foil. The only foil in jail is the foil that wraps Cadbury chocolate on the weekly grocery buy-up. It took me a long time to figure out why some of the young boys always asked for chocolate wrappers. Syringe users recycled empty pen casings into which they placed a sewing needle. A rubber band was then wound up extra tight so that upon release it created enough pressure to puncture the skin and inject the drug.

And for a bit of additional entertainment, a couple of the more technical inmates managed to figure out a way to get the USB ports on some of the older model televisions to work. All the televisions purchased in jail had their USB ports disabled. Once enabled, porn smuggled into jail on USB sticks became an incredibly valuable commodity. Often, lawyers who were authorised to bring laptops and USBs to legal visits would also bring a USB for entertainment. The beauty of this is that no officer is permitted to check the contents of anything of a legal nature. Sitting in a cell with ten other men watching hardcore porn, however, was not my thing, especially knowing that some of them were sex offenders. The screenings were also possible during the day only, as the cells were open and inmates could mix freely in larger numbers and were largely unsupervised.

The Ambush

It was the second Wednesday in May 2009, a day like any other in the office. At some stage, I received a message on my Blackberry that an urgent board meeting had been called for 5 p.m. and everyone was to meet in the boardroom. I let my family know that I would be late home, walked into the boardroom right on time and found that I was the only one there.

After about a twenty-minute wait, closer to 5.30 p.m., my CEO and CFO joined me in the boardroom and started to engage in small talk. As I had worked with both of them for about fifteen years, their behaviour seemed very odd. Not long after, our head of HR and three gentlemen whom I had never seen before walked into the boardroom carrying large boxes that appeared to be documents. Two of the strangers sat down opposite me and introduced themselves as lawyers from one of the country's largest legal firms.

My heart instantly skipped a beat, because I immediately knew what was coming. They proceeded to explain that the boxes of documents contained forensic accounting material relating to the alleged embezzlement of funds. As they launched into the outline of their legal matter, I stopped them and looked at the CEO and CFO, both close friends at the time and simply said, 'I'm sorry, I did it.'

As a matter of course, the lawyers, despite the admission, continued their questioning, asking why and how I did it, how much was involved and whether I had any accomplices. To this day, I don't really remember much other than 'I'm sorry, I did it' coming out of my mouth a number of times. During the inquisition, the lawyers continued to produce mountains of paperwork that the forensic accountants had prepared to prove my guilt. Until that day, I had no clear grasp about how much I had embezzled and was gobsmacked to learn that it was $16.64 million over four years.

At some stage during the questioning, another man walked in the room and introduced himself as a workplace psychologist. Before the lawyers allowed me to leave, my employment was terminated effective immediately and I had to surrender my phone, office keys and company belongings. At some stage, the workplace psychologist came over and, while I can't remember whether I was sitting or standing, I do recall thinking that he had a very well thought out set of questions. He asked about my state of mind, likelihood of self-harm, my intended approach in breaking the news to family and also about my support network, including who I would reach out to for financial and legal help. I have no real recollection of my answers and thought that, given the gravity of the situation, he was there to make sure that I would make it home safely and was not in danger of self-harm.

As I was not permitted to return to my desk to retrieve my personal belongings, I prepared to go home and break the news to my family and loved ones. I remember getting in my car at the office and with the psychologist following my car, made the thirty-minute drive home. Upon arrival, I walked in the house, with the psychologist in tow, and told my wife that I had been just been fired and had stolen over $16 million from the company.

What happened from that point forward is a complete blur, much like the couple of hours before. Extreme emotions, friends and family rushing over and an endless sea of conversation, opinions and advice, propelled by the fact that I was due to front court the next day. There was ample food, drinks and break-out rooms of discussions and strategising about the next steps. By the end of the night and with thanks to those supporters present, I had a lawyer to represent me the next day. I remember just sitting in the lounge room, feeling like I was not really there, having trouble hearing clearly and feeling an uncomfortable pressure in my throat. I was bewildered and felt disconnected from not only myself but also those around me as these huge waves of pain intermittently swept over my entire body, each time leaving me overcome by an almost unbearable sense of despair.

The flood of thoughts, confusion and sensations was making me nauseous and I wondered how on earth I would be able to hold it together. What would become of my world and my family? Would all the people in the house still be in our lives tomorrow or the days after?

Over the years, I have often reflected and openly talked about how being caught actually lifted a huge weight off my shoulders. But that afternoon and into the evening, I can't say that I felt anything except an almost suffocating sense of terror.

To this day, when I see a lawyer carrying legal boxes, it takes me straight back to that confrontation in the boardroom. Later, it also became clear that engaging the psychologist was a legal strategy to determine how I would react in the moment of being caught and, later, behave with my family and the wide, tight-knit Jewish community. The workplace psychologist was likely equally interested in pre-empting the fallout when the magnitude of the fraud filtered through.

Missing Clues

Ten weeks before the ambush in the office, I missed a clue. It was a Sunday morning, twenty-four hours before I was due to fly to the US with my family on our annual holiday. I had taken one of the kids in a stroller for a long walk to a local café. While sitting and relaxing with my coffee and babycino, I got a panicked call from my wife at the time asking me to come home immediately because a bunch of law enforcement officers had pulled up at our house and were knocking on the door. I raced home and, upon arrival, discovered three unmarked white vans and about ten plain-clothes agents, who eventually introduced themselves as immigration officers from Border Security.

Within a matter of minutes of arriving home, things got serious very quickly. The agents formed an arc around the front of the house and then the interrogation started. A senior officer asked if we knew Maria, who they had heard was illegally residing with us. A year earlier, we had employed a young Filipino live-in nanny, but we were confused as the Filipino lady living with us was only known to us as Jane. My first reaction to their questions was an honest denial of knowing who Maria was. I was fully aware that employing a live-in nanny without checking her visa status was not the most responsible thing to do. However, given that she had an Australian bank account and Medicare card, there were no red flags. Besides, I certainly would never ask any other worker, be it an electrician, plumber or builder for their immigration status.

The officers proceeded to show me a photo of the woman they were looking for and it was quite clearly a photo of the Jane we knew, who, unbeknown to us, had entered the country under a false name and passport. Hearing what was going on and while I was being questioned, Jane, who was hiding in another part of the house panicked, jumped the back fence of our house and ran, fearing she would be arrested on the spot. I also went into panic mode and instinctively denied all knowledge of anyone living in our house other than my family. Two of the officers then produced a search warrant to look through the house for Maria. One male and one female officer went from room to room but could not find evidence of anyone other than my family.

As the officers were about to leave, the female officer looked in our backyard and saw a small studio apartment at the side of the house. With a very deliberate look in her face, she asked, "Who lives in that room?"

I responded that our nanny Jane lived there. The officers looked at each other and went to check the studio. Of course, they very quickly realised that Jane was in fact Maria and asked where she was. My wife at the time, aware, but obviously not wanting to disclose that she had jumped the back fence, simply said that Maria had gone for a walk. The officers then very sternly asked us to call 'Jane or Maria' by phone and get her to return immediately, because it would be much better for her that she returned voluntarily than going down the path of forcing a search.

We quickly called Jane and upon explaining the gravity of the situation, she promptly returned to the house. When she arrived, two officers immediately detained her in the kitchen, while a couple of senior officers began formally interviewing me. In hindsight, it was really more of an interrogation, which included a series of threats about the repercussions of harbouring an illegal immigrant punishable by imprisonment and/or a $20,000 fine.

I stayed calm and measured this time and advised the officer that given the federal government had issued Jane/Maria a Medicare card and she managed to open a bank account and had a credit card with a major bank, there was no reason for me to suspect that she was here illegally. Furthermore, I proceeded to ask how it was that they, as officers of the government, allowed it to happen if she was in fact in the country illegally.

Upon hearing my rationale and acknowledging that the system was flawed, the conversation took a complete turn and the hostility receded significantly. I imagine that they believed us and saw that we genuinely had Jane's best interest at heart, especially as two of my children were clinging to her from the moment she arrived back at the house. And so a situation of solidarity presented itself between the officers, ourselves and our nanny. We were advised that we had two options. Firstly, they could take Jane away on the spot to be detained at Villawood Detention Centre for processing and deportation which could take up to three months. Alternatively, we could, right there and then and in front of the officers, purchase a one-way ticket to Manila on the next available flight. Needless to say, I went online and immediately purchased a ticket for a flight leaving three days later.

By this time, the officers knew that we were flying to the US the next day and explained that if Maria failed to board the flight to Manila, she would be taken into custody and it would become quite a hostile deportation process for her and would have ramifications for us too upon return. Once the agents sighted the ticket that had been purchased and upon agreement from all of us to follow through with this alternative, they left our house.

The next morning, as we said our very emotional farewells to Jane, we knew that we would probably never see her again. Our first three days in the US were therefore incredibly stressful and although we trusted Jane, we couldn't be certain what would happen and could only breathe easy once she had boarded the plane. Thankfully, Jane called from the airport just before boarding and we said our goodbyes once more.

About two years into my jail sentence, during one of our nightly phone calls, my kids happily told me that they had just spent the day in Sydney with Jane, who was back in Sydney. It turned out that her name was not Jane or Maria and, as good fortune would have it, she ended up re-entering the country under her real name and real passport and to this day is happily married.

And down the track I also found out that the parties that alerted immigration to pay me a visit were most likely the same that I faced in the boardroom ambush. They likely had stumbled across our nanny's situation in building their case against me. And although our nanny's fate was a direct consequence of my indiscretions, I take great solace in the positive way that her life ultimately turned out.

Programs

Every activity in jail that required inmate participation is called a program. Programs are always run by corrective services employees as opposed to uniformed officers. Every jail has a manager of program services and their role includes the overseeing of all educational and recreational activities, which is essentially anything that happens in the jail that is not discipline related.

I'll never forget, early into my sentence, walking into the library one morning before opening time and finding that the bookshelves had been moved to the side walls, creating a large, open carpeted area. To my amazement, about a dozen inmates were in the middle of a yoga class holding the down dog. I never thought that during my jail term I would see a group of hardened criminals doing yoga, in a library of all places, led by a female civilian yoga instructor. To add to this surreal experience, a sound track of meditative music was playing and the smell of incense filled the room.

It was not uncommon for the jail to receive donations from all types of business across many industries. So when we received a large amount of craft materials, two of the female civilian officers decided that undertaking a basket-weaving course would be in the best interest of inmates wishing to be granted work release status. And for the next six weeks, every Tuesday and Thursday afternoon, I wove colourful baskets with my fellow inmates. The sight of two burly bikies, with cigarettes hanging out their mouth in their attempt to delicately weave baskets makes me laugh to this day.

Another activity which I did not participate in but had great admiration for was watching incredibly talented young Indigenous boys creating amazing artwork and also custom painting baseball caps with traditional Dreamtime stories. One of them, whom I had helped with legal matters and would in turn be paid for with cans of tuna, offered to hand-paint three caps for my three children with unique Dreamtime stories and featuring each of their names. Every year during NAIDOC week, the Indigenous boys would get to exhibit their incredible talent at an external exhibition and some even sold their artwork and had those funds available in their jail account.

My favourite program to participate in was the monthly jail barbecue, which we affectionately called the cook-up. The monthly cook-up was organised and funded by the jail. We had three rusty old barbecues to use and would give them the best clean we could. Every inmate was allowed one chop and two sausages, a few bread rolls and as much coleslaw as they wanted. This roughly equated to eighty chops, double that in sausages, cutting up a couple of hundred rolls and making a few giant tubs of coleslaw.

Given the lack of protein available in our day-to day-diet and, for the most part, having no fresh meat, the smell of the barbecue would instantly take me back to my happy place of freedom, friends and family. It clearly had the same impact on many others as the mood always lifted during this rare jail privilege.

Inmate Delegate Committee (IDC)

One of the few opportunities that inmates have to be heard and to air their concerns by the jail's hierarchy is through the Inmate Delegate Committee (IDC). The boys in the yard would nominate five of their fellow inmates, one from each wing, to represent them at the monthly committee meeting with the jail's management. Within the first six months, I was put forward to join the committee and also act as the secretary. Generally, the secretary's duties included ensuring that all issues were tabled and discussed, and that minutes were prepared and then distributed amongst the inmates in the yard. The challenge of the position of course was to keep the boys in the yard happy by addressing their requests and concerns, while not overstepping the mark with jail management. After all, the secretary was just another inmate. Issues raised every month included the availability of medical care including access to dental and optical, the monthly barbecue, the addition of more nutritional food items on the weekly grocery buy-up, the archaic booking method for visits and the very slow and arduous classification process to lower one's security status to gain entry into the work release program.

Roughly ten to fifteen per cent of the matters raised in

the meetings would be considered in earnest and eventually granted. The monthly barbecue and a more streamlined visiting system, for example, were a result of the IDC meetings. I was requested by the jail governor, also known as the general manager, to maintain a copy of all minutes in a lever arch file in my cell. One morning, during one of the regular cell searches, the female governor and the two next most senior officers, both men, were doing the cell searches themselves, a task normally reserved for lower-ranking officers. One of the male officers was a particularly hard-core disciplinarian, ex Irish military, and most of the boys kept clear of him. On this particular cell search, out of nowhere, he shouted at me, asking why I had a lever arch file with minutes of jail meetings in my cell. He continued to berate me in saying that it was a jail offence and that the ramifications were serious. I, however, kept my cool as I could already predict his next question. And when he asked who had granted authority for the documents to be in my cell, I politely smiled and looked past him at the governor and said, 'Ma'am allowed me.' While his rage and embarrassment built, I opened the folder and showed him the permission note signed by the governor. He then grabbed the folder from me and threw it across my jail cell and stormed off to the next cell.

The officer gave me hell at every opportunity for the next three and a half years. He was so vindictive that he even rostered himself to work on my ultimate day of release to ensure that he was the officer in charge of processing my release. On the day of my release, when I was called into the discharge office to complete the final paperwork, he decided to give me one last bit of 'jail therapy'. As we were sitting and he was pretending to review my paperwork, he proudly announced that some of my paperwork seemed incomplete and that there was no way that I would be released that day. And to my amazement, he also said that there was the unresolved matter of the missing sneakers from almost four years earlier. I let him have his moment before I confidently reminded him that once the courts and parole had granted my release, the matter was above his pay grade. I then got up and told him that I would wait outside until the paperwork was signed and I could walk out of the jail a free man.

I went back to my cell, packed up my years of jail belongings and as a final, albeit passive gesture of contempt for this officer and the whole system, I hid the crappy, overpriced jail television that I had to buy in my duffle bag. An hour later, I was very smoothly and quickly ushered out the door without having to see him again.

Debt and the Gamble

As time in jail is abundant, inmates have to come up with ways to cure their boredom and pass their time. One of the easiest ways to do so is to gamble. Given that there is only access to radio and free to air TV, gambling is done inmate to inmate or clandestinely over the phone at a cost of $2 for six minutes. On any given day, there are at least four different tables around the yard where the boys are playing cards. The most common card game is 41. As there are no gambling chips in jail and gambling is not permitted in any form, there are creative ways to buy in to a table and win the pot. Cans of tuna are the most valuable gambling commodity and, generally, buy in can be anywhere between two to six cans and a good day on the tables can earn the winner thirty to forty cans. The winners had to be careful how much tuna they kept in their cell, as the officers were always checking for surplus food. Therefore, the winner would often lend out some of his tuna to other gamblers with interest. The interest was usually a chocolate bar for every week that the tuna was not repaid.

Needless to say, where there are winners, there are those less fortunate too. The regular losers would often rapidly get into debt, which is one of the worst predicaments in jail. Not paying jail debt generally meant getting a hiding. Those who regularly accumulated a lot of debt would often 'bail out'. Bailing out essentially meant going to the officers and letting them know that your life was in danger, without disclosing why, and requesting transfer to another jail. The reality, however, was that those continually bailing eventually ended up either in a jail where a relative of their debt holder was, or after multiple transfers, ended up at the original jail, where their debt accumulation commenced.

Debt headaches were not only common to gamblers of course, but also those who were desperate for tobacco, but couldn't afford the pouch of White Ox, the tobacco brand of choice in jail.

During football season, there was always a weekly tipping competition that again would revolve around tuna as the currency. Even though all phone calls are monitored, I was always amazed at the code that the boys would come up with to call friends on the outside to place bets on the horses. During visits, they would devise a code for a racetrack so that when they made the phone call, they would simply say the code word to represent the track and then two numbers, one to represent the track and the other the race. For example, Randwick might be called Rumble. Therefore, if the inmate wanted to bet on Race 3, Horse No. 7, they would simply say, 'Rumble 3, 7.' Given that most of the inmates were doing decent sentences, I would always wonder how long it would take them to collect their winnings on the outside, or conversely pay for the losses. The word 'all' would be used for a win and the word 'half' was for a place. The amounts they would actually bet would generally be agreed to during visits.

Gambling had no interest for me but I saw plenty of retribution for unpaid debt. A lot of the young boys that came through the system and had not gambled in their life were considered easy prey and quickly lured by the more experienced inmates to join the tables. Many a time, I would hear the boys on the phone to their loved ones asking for more money on their jail account because they had gone into debt. Occasionally, debts would be cleared with smuggled drugs or prescription meds. Every week on buy-up delivery day when all inmates would line up for their grocery buy-up, those inmates who were owed food debt would hover around the buy-up line to make sure that they were paid their debt before the buyer disappeared into their cell, pretending that they did not have the payback groceries.

For the most part, no tuna was ever placed on a gambling table as a ledger was always kept so that when officers came and did their rounds, no suspicion was raised. There were many occasions where, after visits, the families of inmates who were indebted on the inside would be confronted by the families and friends of those who were owed to pay the debt on the outside.

Jail allows you to see the very worst of mankind and also the very best of mankind, often in the same day. At the worst, it can be someone beaten half to death over something as minor as an unpaid debt, while on the very same day, you can see someone give away their last cigarette to help a friend who is suffering. Such was the pendulum of day-to-day life in jail.

The Daily Blue

It is fair to say that every day, there is at least one fight in the yard, sometimes involving two inmates, sometimes many. I was often confronted when alone and not in the company of those who had my back. When challenged in jail, one has three choices. The first is to fight back, which would inevitably result in both parties being sent to the pound for about a week. The second option is to run from the fight, which would result in being labelled a coward and, as such, easy prey in the yard. And the last tactic is to try and stand your ground and talk your way out. For those who know me well, option three was my absolute course of action every time. During my four years and the countless times I was in such a predicament, my instinct to choose reasoning means that I do not have a major jail fight story on my resume.

The rule in jail was that if you were in a fight and no matter how visibly injured you were, you should never 'dog' on the other party. Sticking to 'I didn't see who hit me' or 'I fell in the shower' when being interviewed to establish what happened was the safest option. Once you were labelled a 'dog' in the yard, the other inmates would turn on you pretty fast and the name-calling would start with 'putrid'.

More often than not, fights broke out over the most mundane incidents, a bump in the yard, cheating on the tables or pushing in line when waiting for the phone. Oddly enough, one of the most violence-triggering aspects of jail life was the phone call. The emotion involved in some phone calls to loved ones, particularly as relationships with those on the outside were tested, often led to very loud and aggressive phone conversations and, as tempers flared, there were consequences. Shouting while on the phone risked waking someone from a nap, possibly drug-induced, and could result in a fist being thrown. Many times, the aggression on the phone call resulted in the handset being smashed, rendering it out of order until fixed and providing another reason for a punch up. Even the language and tone of the caller, often directed towards a woman on the other end, could trigger some of the die-hard long-termers waiting in line to put the aggressor in their place, especially if the person was inside for a domestic violence related crime.

Given the absence of all social media and technology, the good old landline is the only daily connection with the outside world. The emotional rollercoaster with loved ones on the outside, experienced through the maximum six-minute windows, often left inmates desperate to jump the queue so that they could get back on the call while there was time. The phones are turned on at seven a.m. and switched off at nine p.m. Cleverly, the jail programs the phones so that each inmate has to wait at least ten minutes before making another phone call. This tactic serves to avoid the more powerful inmates hogging the phone by intimidating others.

For me, those brief six minutes with my kids was the best part of every day. Given the expense of phone calls, I would try and limit calls to two per day. My kids were always one phone call and the second would be to a friend or family member. I was always acutely aware that it is quite confronting to receive a call from prison. When the recipient answers the call of a jail inmate, the following announcement is immediately heard: 'You are about to receive a phone call from an inmate at X Correctional Centre. Your phone call is monitored and may be recorded. Please hang up now if you do not wish to take the call.' If the call is not connected, there is no real way of knowing if someone in fact rejected it or if the recipient was unavailable. At the end of the pre-recorded message heard by both parties, if nobody is on the other line, the inmate has to wait at least ten minutes before trying again. If in fact, the line for the phones is long, you may miss your chance for connecting that day altogether. The feeling of not speaking to friends and family for a day can put even the most hardened inmates on edge.

There would often be days when the phone lines were conveniently down, making life in the yard very volatile. On those days of high tension, when I was confronted and tested by other inmates, it was even more important for your aggressor to be aware that you would be willing to 'drop them' without a second thought. I absolutely hated having to take on that persona, but sometimes option three of reasoning was simply impractical. The only blemish on my otherwise clear fighting record occurred one day when I was tested relatively early on in my jail-lag. It was a make or break confrontation where the instigator was in a drug-induced rage over nothing. When someone is in this state of mind and appears at your cell door, you can't let them in. In this instance, out of self-preservation, but equally knowing that my standing in the yard would hinge on what I did next, I had to throw the first punch and also the second. Thankfully, that's all it took to put him to the ground, where he stayed until the next roll call four hours later. Perhaps it was my punches or the drugs in his system, but he slept soundly on the floor the entire time.

Possibly the most brutal fight I witnessed was during a game of volleyball, during which an Australian inmate called a Middle Eastern inmate a terrorist. The reaction was instant. Within a matter of seconds, about a dozen guys were 'punching on'. The two main protagonists who started the brawl were completely covered in blood, eyes swollen shut, teeth literally knocked out, lips split wide open and knuckles red raw from flesh on flesh. It's incredible how much physical damage can be inflicted in just over a minute. Men in utter rage, no control, no rules or referee and nothing to lose. When the officers came to the yard, nobody gave up anyone, but in observing the injuries, the perpetrators in this case were obvious. They were quickly taken to the pound for a week of solitary holiday.

Jail life has little room for grudges and as soon as the boys were released from the pound, they shook hands and moved on as if nothing had happened. A fight of such a scale would not only mean that the men would end up in the pound, but they were also punished with a loss of jail privileges including not being allowed to buy groceries for a month. In this particular case, the hardest part was that, as both the fighters were smokers, it also meant four weeks of no tobacco, as that was part of the weekly grocery options. Of course, it meant that to smoke they would have to 'borrow' a pouch or two to get through the four-week period, feeding the jail economy of debt and payback.

Civil Proceedings

My journey through the legal system passed through a number of courts. It started with civil proceedings in the NSW Supreme Court before segueing into the Federal Court, which oversees bankruptcy proceedings, and finishing with the District Court of NSW to undertake criminal proceedings.

The morning after I was found out and news broke to my family and friends, I was summoned to attend court. All the male supporters who had been at my house the night before came to court that first day. Before the hearing, I sat outside the courthouse in a café with my supporters. I was surprised at how many of them encouraged me to get on the first plane out of the country and run. Others of course told me to man up and take it on the chin. In my view, there really was only one course of action. And therefore, even though I was physically able to travel early on, at no point in the entire process did I contemplate running away. I had spent so long living the lie of two lives that putting my hand up and owning my actions was the only option.

Civil proceedings, unlike criminal proceedings, are quite technical and often involve adjournments, mediation and negotiations. On the first day in court, my former employer's legal team managed to obtain an order freezing all my assets while they were building the case. This meant that all my bank accounts and credit cards linked to my accounts were frozen and a caveat had been placed over my house. In addition, the freezing order forbade me from disposing of any existing assets including shares, jewellery and personal effects. It was up to my legal team to negotiate a living allowance while proceedings took place with the opposing side. In the end, the most they would allow to be released each week was $600. The only thing that they could not freeze was my American Express Card. I used the remaining credit on this to pre-pay both my daughters' school fees for the rest of the year.

On around day four of the civil proceedings, I was in the mediation room with the opposing legal teams. They were insistent that I surrender my passport as they believed that I was a flight risk. As I had decided to tell the truth and not run, I had no issue with it, but reminded them that I was not a flight risk but I believed my business partner to be. When we returned to the courthouse after the meeting, the opposing legal team stood up and let the judge know that they had reached an agreement for me to surrender my passport. I remember the judge looking at me and then the opposing lawyer and then chastising him for arranging a passport surrender as it was the duty of the judge and the courts. He then politely asked me whether I agree to surrender my passport. Upon agreeing, and as is the case in NSW courts, I had twenty-four hours to produce and surrender it.

During that first week of court, I grabbed the opportunity one day to go the Westpac bank in my local area to withdraw my $600 weekly allowance in cash. As I stood in the line, I happened to turn round and standing directly behind me was the chairman and founder of the company that I was now in court proceedings with. Of all people. Just a few a weeks ago, I was part of his team. My wave of shame was intense and overpowering. Lining up to get my allowance and imagining him watching was utterly embarrassing. Another haunting memory of those days is the irony that we still lived in a beautiful house, but came home daily to anonymous food packages on our doorstep.

On my first day in court, as I listened to the lawyers argue, it quickly became evident that the house and pretty much everything would be repossessed and sold. The reality of not knowing where we were going to live, what I would do for a living and how I would feed my family completely froze me. It's one of those moments that even now makes me feel sick. As the civil proceedings rolled on and the media became involved, the number of our supporters also dwindled. Judgements had been made, friendships were ending and a new reality was setting in. I could already tell at that early stage who would stick by me and who would disappear. To this day, those who stuck by me remain my staunchest supporters and friends.

The process of civil proceedings in general is quite intimate but cold. The judge sits at his table. There is a witness dock and a table for each of the prosecutors and defendants. My hearing was in a very small courtroom with not much room for supporters. My legal team pointed out to me early on that any strangers in the back row would most likely be the media. I learnt that there was one particular journalist who had decided that she would make a name for themselves from my case. And as a result, each morning after the previous day's proceedings, I was petrified as to what she would publish in the paper.

It soon became apparent that the strange cars parked in my street and following my family were also the media. Possibly one of the most humiliating days of the entire court process was the day tow trucks arrived to repossess the family cars. The media made sure that there were plenty of lenses to capture the moment of course. Only now am I able to smile at a gossip column byline that exclaimed, 'Oh no, not the Range Rover.' The true power of the media when you are newsworthy was made even more clear one night when the aforementioned journalist called my house late and demanded a photo of me for publication the next day. She proceeded to tell me that should I fail to send a photo, she would use a stock photo that included my children and, in ending the call, gave me one hour to comply. Within ten minutes, I emailed the journalist a photo that ended up accompanying the next day's article.

Unlike criminal proceedings, civil proceedings have no bailiff, officers of the court, or any barriers of entry and exit. The purpose of them is to attempt to reach a financial judgement against the defendant. The judgement can be fought and denied, consented to with full admission of guilt, or consented to without admissions, the latter meaning that the defendant consents to all civil charges against them but without any formal admission of guilt. In cases of the magnitude that mine was, civil proceedings could drag on for many months, debating the minutiae of the law, with the best possible outcome for all parties being to consent to a judgement without admissions. This was the path my team agreed to with the prosecuting team and meant a judgement of $16.64 million plus costs being awarded against me, resulting in about $18 million in total.

When I ultimately found myself in the dock during the civil trial, I was advised, as is the norm, to always ensure that questions asked of me were answered with a yes or no, or 'I do not wish to answer that question as it may incriminate me.' At its most basic, the civil process is about lawyers dancing to see which party can achieve the best result. Given that my former employer had spent over $750,000 on forensic accountants and many thousands of dollars on lawyers by this point, the civil proceedings really just serve as a process for agreeing on the amount that the judgement would ultimately be consented to. I remember many questions being asked around what I had spent the misappropriated funds on and where those funds were now. Again, unlike criminal proceedings, the questions of motive do not come into play. When asked about the whereabouts of the money or its use, my answer remained the same each time. I explained that the moneys were poured into propping up my three struggling private businesses. The opposing legal team, knowing the media was present, was intent on painting a picture that many millions were hidden in a proverbial mattress. The reality, however, was not even close.

My civil case ended up being two weeks long and its conclusion was very anticlimactic. Once I had consented to the judgement without admission and the judge agreed to the plea, I was free to go, with no immediate criminal consequence. However, it did trigger the courts to force the sale of the house and cars. An agent was immediately appointed and all non-mortgaged value was taken by the court. As part of the freezing orders, I could no longer maintain lease payments on the family cars.

Moving On

Selling the family home was a very public process. We chose agents who we trusted would bring the greatest price, not because we could profit in any way, but to maximise the amount that my former employers could recoup. Once again, the media made sure that they kept a close eye on the proceedings. It was quite clear that most potential purchasers were aware of the reason for the sale and were hunting for a bargain. Ultimately, the house sold for $500,000 less than market expectations and there was nothing that could be done to negotiate up as the creditors were also after a quick sale.

During the period of settlement, we made the decision to relocate from life under the microscope to a more anonymous location on Sydney's North Shore. It was actually very comforting to move to an area with relative anonymity. I was not a complete stranger to our new neighbourhood, though, as our next home was only a few streets away from the high school I graduated from.

Around this time, one of my friends in real estate suggested that, given my extensive background in property, I should move into residential real estate and join her and her husband in their relatively new agency on the Northern

Beaches. Confident that I could sell, the offer of a job outside the bubble of Sydney's East, and of course the ability to support my family, made me jump at the chance.

Three days later, I was dressed in a suit again. However, this time it was for my first day of work as a real estate agent in training. Nobody at the Northern Beaches agency knew who I was, or thankfully had read about my case in the media. In 2009, Googling everyone was not as prevalent as it is today. Regardless, it was decided that although I would get my certificate of registration to be an agent, the name I went by at the agency would be my first and second name only, omitting my last name on property advertising.

Working in real estate gave me the opportunity to reinvent myself and learn something new. I did my best to excel in the world of finding listings and selling properties and was incredibly grateful for the opportunity and challenge of chasing deals. Moreover, this also provided a welcome distraction from the trauma of the civil proceedings. To this day, I do not believe that any of my real estate clients knew about me or my past, despite having my photograph on many billboards around the Northern Beaches.

Starting out in real estate is not the most financially rewarding occupation as it takes a while for your commissions to offset the base salary credit system, but I was determined to gain traction as quickly as possible.

As a result of the judgement, I was faced with a formal court debt of over $18 million and my former employer was now able to commence bankruptcy proceedings in the Federal Court. This involved a court-appointed trustee investigating and locating any assets that might not have been declared in the civil proceedings. Quite early on, it became evident to the trustee that there were no further assets to find, which I imagine was extremely disappointing to my former employers given that they went to the trouble of issuing a formal 'cease and desist,' even when we tried to hold a garage sale to offload unwanted household items and toys. In Australia, once the investigative work of the trustee is completed and formal bankruptcy filings are undertaken, the Federal Court declares you bankrupt and, assuming conditions of bankruptcy are not breached, the period of bankruptcy lasts three years. During that time, one cannot take on any financial responsibilities – for example, loans of any kind – nor can you own any assets, including a vehicle of greater value than $6,000.

I was happy to be gainfully employed at the agency and tried to continue to create as normal a life as possible for my family. However, feelings of impending doom were with me most of the time. The end of my civil proceedings meant that life was now a waiting game as to when criminal charges would be brought against me.

After about six months at the agency, as I was driving to view a new potential listing in Beacon Hill, my phone rang. The call was from a man who introduced himself as Detective Summer from the NSW Fraud Squad, attached to Strikeforce Swordfish set up as a result of my civil proceedings. He casually said that they would like me to go in for a chat. Even though I had been anticipating a call of this nature, I took a moment and advised that I have next Wednesday off and whether it was OK to come into the station at that time. The detective casually responded that there was no rush and whenever it suited was fine. I then asked if I needed to bring a lawyer. The response was relaxed once again, saying that it was up to me, as it was just a chat.

My thinking at the time was that the matter could not be too serious as the request and timing of the meeting were casually presented. After the detective and I agreed to meet the following Wednesday at ten a.m. for the chat, I immediately called my lawyer and he rightly insisted on accompanying me. Over the forthcoming six days, I continued as normal at work while my lawyer and confidantes bounced around ideas regarding the best and worst case scenarios of the meeting. We agreed that given the casual nature of the invitation, I was in no imminent criminal danger. Regardless, I hardly slept during the ensuing nights.

The Sword of Damocles

It was the beginning of November 2009 and the weather the following Wednesday was very warm. My attire was smart casual in dress pants, dress shoes and a nice shirt. I walked into Surry Hills Police Station with my lawyer and introduced myself to the officer at the front desk.

Within two minutes, Detective Summer and his colleague walked to the reception desk to meet me and the first words they spoke were, "Mr Simon Feldman, we are formally charging you with 227 counts of 176a officer defraud or cheat. You are now under arrest in respect to these charges."

I was immediately asked to surrender all my personal belongings and consent to a formal interview. At this point, my lawyer rightfully asked to consult with his client privately and we were led to the formal interview room and left alone for a few minutes. During this time, I was instructed by my lawyer to consent to the interview and respond to questions with 'I do not wish to answer this question.' My lawyer and I allowed the police back into the interview room and the formal interview began.

Pretty much as depicted in the movies, I was advised that the interview would be recorded and that any evidence might be used against me in court. To this day, I can still hear the click of the recording machine. The officers asked more questions than I can remember and it became quite clear that the investigation was a cut and paste of the civil proceedings. At the conclusion of the interview, I was placed in a holding cell for processing. The holding cell, which is essentially a chair in a cage, was located in front of the reception desk and fully visible to all. I remember thinking that it looked like a phone booth but with bars. I was permitted to use the phone to let family know of my whereabouts. My lawyer sat with me for what seemed like hours and I next recall being taken up to the courthouse the following day. I had been locked up in the holding cell for about sixteen hours, in and out of sleep.

Still wearing my clothes from the previous day, I was taken upstairs for a formal bail hearing. At this point, I had no barrister and as such it was up to my lawyer to negotiate bail. During the initial bail hearing, the police painted a very sombre picture to the judge, implying that I was hiding millions of dollars. Consequently, this bail hearing resulted in my bail terms being $500,000 in cash and surrender of my passport. I certainly did not have that kind of money and my passport had already been surrendered during the civil case and handed to the Bankruptcy Trustee.

Once bail is set, the individual is formally held in the custody of Corrective Services until the conditions of bail are met, which in my case was providing the money and passport. And so this point marked the beginning of my journey to lock-up and was my first visit to the little-known hellhole that is the Corrective Services run Surry Hills cells underneath Hyde Park.

My lawyer had managed to negotiate a reduction in the monetary amount to $250,000. I was very fortunate that my incredible Perth-based aunts, my late mother's sisters, agreed to put up the bail security. What no one expected, however, was that the process of having the surety arranged across another state and jurisdiction meant that it took about three weeks of bureaucracy for me to be released on bail. I was eventually released at ten p.m. on a Sunday night in late November.

While awaiting bail, I spent the three weeks between the Surry Hills cells and MRRC (Metropolitan Remand and Reception Centre) at Silverwater. Upon arrival at MRRC, we were herded out of a prison truck and into giant holding pens with others of similar security status. The wait in the holding pens could be anywhere from three to ten hours. Each holds up to twenty people to one toilet. Everyone seems to be on edge and only those inmates who have been through the system before know what is going on.

I sat in the corner of the pen alone, too scared to use the toilet, too scared to make eye contact and unsure of what being processed actually meant. I was eventually taken to another holding area alone where all the civilian clothes that I was wearing were taken and I was given my first set of prison greens. They included green shorts, green T-shirts, green socks and Velcro Dunlop Volleys. I then had to stand in front of a camera to be photographed for my prison ID card and was then taken for an interview where my safety and security levels were assessed.

Upon evaluation, Corrective Services informed me that due to the profile and nature of my crime, as well as my religion and appearance, it was in my best interest and their duty of care that I be classified as a limited association (LA) inmate. I was immediately taken to the segregation cells in what was known as the Darcy Pod. Darcy Pod consisted of three areas that I was aware of. Darcy 1 housed the segregation cells and Darcy 2 and 3 were multilevel holding cells. I was initially placed in a segregation cell alone for one week before being moved to the general cells.

Segro

While in Darcy 1 segregation, also called 'segro', I was housed in a row of ten cells that, although joined, were designed so that inmates could not physically interact or see each other. The front door of each cell was of thick metal with a small glass window and a drop-down flap to communicate. The rear of the cell was a semi-open area with a back area consisting of bars for a roof and a wall. Due to the open bars at the rear of the cell, inmates were able to verbally communicate or pass things between cells, but could not see each other or cross paths.

As it happened, my weeks at Darcy 1 in 2009 coincided with the arrest of a number of members of a well-publicised bikie gang as a result of their involvement in an airport riot and murder. My neighbours during my first stay in a regular jail, as opposed to a holding cell, were therefore seven high-profile Muslim gang members, one ex police officer and one young boy who was the youngest brother of the founding members of a South Sydney Beach Crew.

Surrounded by gang members who somehow knew all about me and, upon my arrival, took every opportunity to make sure that I went through a verbal initiation process, was quite a learning curve. From day one, they referred to me as 'the Jew' and were generally disparaging. A couple of days into my stay, they were all reciting rap songs at the top of their voice. At one point, the well known and now deceased leader of the gang jokingly shouted to me saying that he doubted I had ever heard of the tunes they were enjoying. I took the opportunity to inject some humour into my reply and take the gamble that it might, in some minor way, endear me to this crowd. Therefore, my reply to him was 'Of course I do, I am the Notorious J.E.W!' What made this even more relevant was that the artist that they were impersonating was called Notorious B.I.G. The entire row of cells erupted into laughter and from that moment on, there was a mutual respect that broke the ice and eased the aggression. Ironically, both the artist Notorious B.I.G and the gang leader next to me shared the same fate of being assassinated by a hail of bullets while in their car.

As observant Muslims, my neighbours prayed five times a day and would often write notes and share a prayer book between them. The only way to get notes and the prayer book between cells was to pass it down the line along the outside bars. As my cell was wedged in the middle, I not only found myself in the middle of the game of pass the parcel but, given our peace treaty, I also had very little choice other than to participate in the forbidden activity.

When I was eventually relocated to the general cells in Darcy 2 and 3, still awaiting bail to be posted, I got my first taste of how slowly time passes in jail. Every day is exactly the same. I was lucky that I only spent three weeks on remand and I honestly do not know how others get through endless months while fighting their case. The only reason I wanted bail was that I naively thought bail meant I was going to be out for a few months and that would give me the chance to put my affairs in order and finalise the court case as I had made the decision to plead guilty. I assumed that the entire legal process would be a matter of months. An acquaintance I met while in custody, however, warned me that sometimes getting bail was a curse, because if a court case dragged on, any time out on bail, unlike time on remand, is not taken off your ultimate sentence. In my situation, the court case dragged on for fifteen months and every time I went to court during that time, and I lost count of the number of court appearances, the overwhelming fear that my bail could be revoked and a sentence handed down at any moment was ever present.

Once bail was posted, I was taken from my cell on a Sunday night and released to my family. During the forty-minute drive home, I looked out the window of the car as if seeing everything for the first time. I noticed colours, every smell and, instead of feeling free, all I could think about was the day that I would have to go back into custody. As I got home late that night, I held my kids and then curled up into a ball in my bed and fell asleep properly for the first time in weeks. Being on such high alert over that time completely drained me.

I woke the next morning knowing that my freedom was limited, with no idea about what lay ahead, but happy to no longer be locked up. Part of my bail conditions was reporting twice weekly to Hornsby Police Station at designated times. This started the conditioning for jail life to come. I recall delaying my bail check-in to the evening one day and had fallen asleep on the couch only to wake twenty minutes before my bail check-in time closed. The fear of being late was totally overwhelming because I knew that if I was one minute late, it would mean breach of bail and I would be taken into custody, not to mention the reality that my family would have forfeited their bail money.

The bail process itself is very cut and dry in NSW as I imagine it would be elsewhere too. Even a simple breach, such as missing a police check-in, will result in being taken into custody until a breach of bail hearing is arranged. At such a hearing, one would need to argue if the breach was accidental, be it a late check-in by a matter of minutes or whether it was something more premeditated such as using illegal substances. The bail judge is the sole arbitrator whether to declare breach of bail, triggering bail to be withdrawn, or rule the breach minor and as such allowing bail to be continued.

The week after I was released from remand, my lawyer suggested that, until I was sentenced, I should find a job once more, not only to keep my mind occupied, but also to show the courts that I was a contributing member of society, which is a mitigating factor. Obviously, returning to work in real estate was not an option while on parole. Regardless of how long it would be before I was back in jail, the idea of earning money and keeping myself busy sounded sensible.

In search of a job once again, I walked down to the local shops in our new neighbourhood and saw a few job advertisements with detachable phone numbers. The ad that got my attention was one that advertised the opportunity to earn $700 cash per week, working in a local call centre. I rang the number and had an interview the next day. An hour after arriving for the interview, I started work tasked with selling government-funded energy-saving appraisals to home owners. By the end of the first week, I was the top-selling salesman and by the third week, I was the pseudo-manager of the call centre.

Not surprisingly, the owner of the call centre, Jonty, realised that there was more to me than met the eye. I took the gamble and showed him the last newspaper article written about me. It made no difference to him whatsoever and only kickstarted the friendship that we still have today. He even accompanied me to court every day of my criminal hearings and visited me in jail. We even tried to get a new business off the ground upon my release.

The Real Rake

A criminal court case in the NSW district Court is far from a quick and logical process. With the help of my family, I was fortunate enough to secure the services of the ever colourful and flamboyant Charles Waterstreet. Charles was truly remarkable in fighting my case, because unfortunately, one simply does not walk into a courtroom to plead guilty in order to secure a speedy sentencing.

As I would learn over the coming months, the criminal process has many layers. It involves a defendant chasing a prosecutor for their brief of evidence which is essentially the prosecutorial evidence trail and can take several months. In the meantime, the defendant has to make several court appearances, generally referred to as motion hearings, which could take hours and sometimes just five minutes in court, but regardless incur a full day's cost of legal fees. In addition to the motion hearings, the process includes multiple hearings where evidence is submitted including references, psychiatric reports and any other material relevant to mitigating circumstances.

In addition, personnel and their availability also come into play as a key part of the process. In my case, members of the DPP were unavailable due to maternity, sick and long service leave and those absences necessitated the judge to find other openings in her legal calendar. Furthermore, the DPP also wanted to cross-examine me and a number of people who had provided character references on the stand to see if they could extract any additional unknown facts that they could attach to the case.

Despite the number of charges and in order to reduce the term of one's sentence, the role of a barrister is to reduce the number of charges to as few as possible. Therefore, the next step was for both legal sides to negotiate how many of the 227 charges I would formally plead guilty to. It would namely have to be a lengthy and costly exercise for the DPP to prove guilt on all 227 charges and as such a reduced amount of charges was the norm. Despite this process, all charges not pleaded on still appear on what is called a Form 1. Charges on a Form 1 are not sentenced on, but they contribute to the totality of the judge's decision in sentencing.

Every court event was a revolving door of reporters, legal observers and assorted family and friends. I was heavily medicated throughout the criminal hearing as my psychiatrist appointed by my legal team had prescribed a high dose of anti-anxiety medication, one of the side effects of which was that I was not up or down but a solid midline shell incapable of much emotion. I have been told that Charles Waterstreet was very entertaining and talented while acting in my defence. However, I was anaesthetised to most of the court machinations.

The remarkable skill of Charles was not only his incredible legal nous, but credit must also be given to his extraordinary ability to command the attention of everyone in the courtroom. Yet despite his flamboyant theatrics, he took all the time needed to educate me about the legal process at every step of the way and he was also surprisingly nurturing, with a hint of cheeky wit at all times. I could easily understand how women were enamoured by him and judging by his chambers the feeling was mutual, as the walls there were covered in beautiful artwork depicting mostly naked women. Walking into his rooms, despite the duress I was under, was a complete distraction to my legal reality. In spite of being so organised and switched on in court, his place of work was quite the opposite with boxes, papers and files everywhere. Rightly or wrongly, I believe that the outcome of my case was not solely attributable to Charles's legal manoeuvres. He was also shown tremendous respect throughout the court system and I think that that played a part in the fairness with which my case was tried.

Due Process

From the outset, Charles Waterstreet was very clear that the best way to mitigate any top line sentencing was to firstly plead guilty at the earliest opportunity, secondly to assist the court with any matters relating to any co-offenders, and thirdly to produce one's own list of mitigating circumstances. The terminology of top for maximum and bottom for minimum line sentencing in a criminal court refers to the maximum and minimum periods in a custodial sentence. If the top sentence is eight years and the bottom is five years, this translates to a maximum prison term of eight years with a minimum of five years served, at which point one is eligible for parole, provided that the parole authority is satisfied that time in jail has minimised the risk of reoffending and the offending behaviour has been addressed. In fact, one of the first questions asked in jail by other inmates is always 'What did you get on the top and what did you get on the bottom.' It was almost a way of breaking the ice with newly acquainted inmates while at the same time not breaking a cardinal rule of asking, 'What are you in for?'

In my proceedings, I pleaded guilty at the earliest opportunity, not only because of the legal directive, but also because I saw no reason to waste people's time or taxpayers' and my family's money on a matter that I was guilty of. The maximum discount, although not official but standard practice, for fully cooperating in the court process, including the early guilty plea, is a twenty-five per cent discount on the ultimate sentence. When one then adds their own mitigating circumstances, this can mean up to a thirty-five per cent or more reduction of the top line sentence. The net result in my case was that the maximum ten years I could have received on top was reduced to six and a half years, of which I served four.

The NSW Criminal Court is unlike the criminal court system in the US, where sentences for financial and many other crimes are run consecutively as opposed to concurrently. In my case, had I been in the US, I could have been looking at 130 years of imprisonment on the basis of my guilty pleas.

I remember conducting my own research into what might occur during sentencing by spending hours and hours trawling online case histories and trying to match charge number '176a officer defraud or cheat' to amounts of money in question and comparing possible mitigating circumstances. My own 'bush lawyer' appraisal of my destiny had me spending five to six years in jail as opposed to the four years I ultimately received.

From the very outset, there were a number of legal options that I could have pursued and there was certainly no lack of opinions from those around me. These varied from falling on my sword with dignity, to bringing others down with me as well, even if unrelated to my crime. For me, the decision to own my mistakes was the only way forward. I was only too aware of the collateral damage of my actions and therefore was intent on focusing on dealing with the consequences with as much decency as possible. And over the years, many people have commended my handling of proceedings, jail and life thereafter. While this validation is always satisfying to receive, it will always serve as a reminder of my lowest of low and the road that I have been walking ever since.

Sentencing

After fourteen months of proceedings, a sentencing date was finally set and I decided that I wanted to be 100 per cent mentally present and not medicated when I attended the hearing. Therefore, about four or five days before the slated sentencing date, I stopped cold turkey on all medication without telling anyone and without seeking medical guidance. As someone who had never been on medication previously, I was not aware that it could cause any possible ramifications.

And so it happened that about two days after I stopped taking my medication, I got up in the morning, left the house and for the next twenty-four hours, no one knew where I was or what I had done. My family notified the police as well as local medical services and I was eventually discovered in a dishevelled and barely conscious state in the bushes at the back of my house. An ambulance took me to the emergency psychiatric ward (PEC) at Hornsby Hospital and I was admitted. Accordingly, my legal team successfully requested a four-week delay in my sentencing so that my mental health could be assessed.

Being in a psychiatric unit for observation was both surreal and humiliating. The irresponsibility of stopping the medication, especially without medical supervision, was made abundantly clear. I spent three days in the PEC and was then discharged and went home. I did not have any recollection of what had happened during the time I was missing and the doctors concluded that I must have blacked out. Naturally, the episode also significantly impacted my family and friends and over the ensuing weeks, I tried to put everyone's mind at ease that I was not having a breakdown.

Before long, the new and final sentencing hearing approached and was held on a Friday morning, late in February. I vividly recall the judge, in what I was later told to be a unique statement, reminding me that a custodial sentence was to be handed down on the Monday and that I would not be going home for some time. Back on medication, I spent that weekend numb, watching my family go about their normal day to day life, a life that I knew I would not be part of in a few days' time. It's hard to reflect on my thoughts that weekend. Dealing with the consequences of my crime had become a non-negotiable part of my existence and, difficult as that was, I still had a life. But I still had the joy of being around my children and being part of their world.

Friends and family called and visited without raising the elephant in the room. Looking back, I think I still must have been in a state of denial, because I recall a sense of hope that the judge would perhaps have a change of heart over the weekend. I will never know what it must have been like for my kids when they said farewell to me as I left for court on that final Monday morning.

On Monday, with my friends and family in the back of

the courtroom, I stood in front of the judge as he handed down his sentence. My mind was not as sharp as normal in trying to understand the three separate concurrent sentences that the judge handed down. He had grouped four charges into each of the three sentences to cover the twelve I had pleaded guilty to. When he finished speaking, I looked at Charles Waterstreet for a translation. A six and a half year sentence, serving a minimum of four. Although I probably expected a harsher outcome, I still stood shell-shocked at the reality of years in jail. The judge allowed me to farewell my family and friends before I was cuffed and taken below to the Surry Hills holding cells.

Visits

Visits are the most bittersweet part of jail life. All jail visits occur on the weekend and are an opportunity to physically connect with family and friends and in some way feel part of the outside world. Visits take place in a very strict and supervised environment where even visitors are often treated like criminals by virtue of association. Visitors must not only run the gauntlet of unfriendly and unhelpful administrative staff when trying to book the visit, but they also, upon arrival at the jail, have to run through the hoops of presenting four different kinds of identification. Once having passed through security, they must also surrender their phone, wallet and keys. Aside from the clothing they are wearing, they are only permitted to carry prescription glasses and $20 in gold coins for the vending machine.

    The visiting environment itself is a melting pot of family, partners, screaming kids, lawyers, pastoral visitors and friends. Inmates on good behaviour are permitted to have what is called a contact visit. This means sitting at a table with four chairs where it is possible, within reason, to hold hands or hug loved ones. Those not on good behaviour are only permitted non-contact or box visits. A box visit is exactly as it sounds. An inmate sits in a perforated Perspex box where they can see but never touch their visitors. I was always torn between joy and shame during visits. There was the elation of seeing family and friends, but always tinged with shame sitting there in jail greens as a constant reminder of my reality. One of the hardest things was when my kids came to visit and seeing all of them, even my three-year-old son, having to be swiped with a metal detector as if they were smuggling contraband to me.

Sitting with my family during visits and sharing the space with murderers, sex offenders, drug dealers and those guilty of many other crimes was disturbing and added to my guilt and feelings of shame. The mixing of my jail life and outside life in the small surrounds of that room was one I would often think about back in my cell. The harsh reality of the very best part of my life mixing with the very worst was a humbling reality check.

To avoid smuggling of contraband, visitors in NSW jails are not permitted to bring anything as a gift for an inmate other than underwear in its original packaging. The tradition of visits was that visitors would feed as many of their $20 of coins as possible to the vending machine to fuel the inmate with as much chocolate and soft drinks as possible because those treats were mostly too expensive on the weekly grocery buy-up.

Given the high profile of some of the inmates at my jail, security cameras were forbidden. As a result, officers would sit on chairs as close as possible to inmates they suspected of smuggling contraband and to stop any over amorous behaviour. In my jail, even in the most extreme of summer heat, inmates were required to wear long tracksuit pants. The reason was to discourage inappropriate touching under the table.

Jail visits turned out to be a real eye opener to who my real friends were. Aside from my family and close circle of friends, I was often surprised by random visitors who came to see me, including people I had not seen for a long time, even on the outside. There were also interstate and overseas family and friends, as well as former business acquaintances. It was often hard to contain my emotions when someone unexpected showed up. In fact, I was often so humbled that I felt guilty that they had to come to a jail to see me. I have never discounted the impact that all this has had on those who chose to come to a jail. Many of my friends remind me to this day of how poorly they were treated on arrival and departure by prison officers, but knew not to complain at the time as it would only blow back on me.

I am forever grateful to the amazing not-for-profit organisation SHINE for kids. This volunteer-led organisation was set up to build a bridge between inmates and their children to overcome the difficult family dynamic of having a parent in jail. Every twenty-eight days, SHINE would organise a social worker, always the same amazing man, to bring my kids to spend three hours with me. The visits would be the only times I saw my children during the first three years of my sentence.

This visiting environment was a stark contrast to the one on remand at MRRC where all inmates, due to being unsentenced and thus deemed maximum security, had to wear boiler suits during every visit. In preparation for remand visits, inmates would be taken to a screening room to be strip searched to their underwear and given a canvas onesie boiler suit which zipped at the back. Depending on their risk rating, they would either wear white or orange and those of extreme high risk would also have to be shackled around their wrist and ankles. Visitors as well as inmates in a remand centre are required to have retina ID verification. This is intended to stop inmate substitution and banned visitors from visiting. I limited my visitors while on remand to close family and legal representation only, because the environment was simply too confronting for everyone.

The Primal Urge

One of the most frequent questions I get asked about is how much sex, consensual or non-consensual, there is in a male jail. I can only answer from my experience at Silverwater Correctional Centre and, in my case, through the eyes of a minimum-security inmate. Inmates who had experienced both maximum and medium security jails did tell me that the degree of sexual activity is different between jails and varying security levels.

The denial of intimacy and human touch would be one of the toughest aspects of jail for most. When you also add boredom, drug use, egos and favours, sex in its many forms is very much part of jail life. Although I chose to steer clear of this subculture, I witnessed sexual activities under a wide range of circumstances.

My first experience happened in the first few months of my sentence. The first wing that I was housed in oddly shared the same rear security wall as the women's jail. Every night after lock-in, the younger boys in my wing would start yelling and talking at the top their voice to women on the other side of the wall. The aim was always to be as crude as possible. I was in complete shock not only at the things I heard, but also at the fact that both sides of the fence would openly give out their name and jail identification numbers (MIN). And once details were exchanged, letters would start to flow between men and women who had never actually met or seen each other before. While I am no prude, I was absolutely floored by the content of the letters by both sides. I remember reading a letter from a female inmate to another male inmate and learning in explicit detail about the sexual conduct within the female jail. I was also educated in the art of a jail-made dildo. The taping together of multiple toothbrushes and the availability of deodorant and shampoo bottles made for an interesting collection of home-made sex toys. Conversely, I was astounded to discover that one of the younger men who had a female pen pal on the other side would always ejaculate on his letter before posting it.

The undercurrent of sexual frustration that could not be requited naturally fuelled the popular time-killing activity of constant masturbation. The many openly discussed incarnations used to heighten the experience makes me shudder to this day and ranged from self-piercings to marbles being placed in the male shaft.

TV watching was limited to free to air, and no cable or streaming was available. One night per week, the officers would play a video through the jail's TV station and, for the most part, it would be an old action movie. On a few occasions, a generous officer would 'accidentally' broadcast adult content through the jail channel to entertain the lads. It was always of the absolute lowest quality video and gave the experience of watching a coin-operated porn reel at Kings Cross in the 1980s.

Suffice to say, it did not surprise me to find out that many married or straight men in jail would engage in sexual activities with other inmates. Such inmates would generally be referred to as being 'gay for the stay' and, quite often, those with a longer sentence would jokingly use the adage 'any hole is a goal'. It was difficult to see male inmates being visited by their wives and kids on weekends, while knowing what was happening behind closed cell doors the rest of the time.

Of course, not every inmate was married or had a significant other. The fascination with bad boys is very real and it seems that females of all walks of life are drawn to a man in jail. Perhaps it's the birds with broken wing syndrome or just a fascination with someone on the wrong side of the law. I am not sure how the women and girls found these inmates, but regardless, there was never a shortage of blossoming romances during visits. Although not an ideal place to be courting, the festival of pheromones was unavoidable. And so unsurprisingly, this would manifest itself in a line-up of scantily clad women driving the guys crazy. Although hand holding and a small kiss were permitted, the hands of the men were often exploring the nether regions of their female suitors. On one such occasion, a lady attempted to reciprocate by sliding her hand up the male inmate's shorts. Unfortunately, this ruse was discovered and the punishment for not only that inmate but, from that time forward, was that all inmates were required to wear long tracksuit pants even in the most extreme of summer heat. Sitting in thick fleece trackpants on a hot day for a couple of hours is a mood killer, no matter the temptation.

It never ceased to break my heart when I witnessed some of the younger boys with drug addictions and limited jail funds trading sexual favours as currency for drugs, tobacco, food and other necessities. Of course, it often meant that such vulnerable young men were at the behest of larger and stronger men and were therefore often taken advantage of.

The only opportunity for intimacy outside of the jail yard during one's sentence was for those inmates lucky enough to take part in the works release program. In such instances, some would take a risk and organise sexual liaisons either at their workplace or arrange clandestine rendezvous en route to or from work. While the upside is obvious, the downside, should one be caught, was the immediate cancellation of all leave programs and most in-jail privileges for the individual. For those serving a long sentence, the risk was outweighed by the reward. Until they were caught of course.

Is Anyone Spared, I Wonder

A little over a year into my sentence, I found myself sharing a cell with a large, seasoned Slavic inmate, easily weighing over 100 kilograms. At that stage, I was in a wing that housed C2 inmates, which meant that, while the wing door was locked at night, the individual cell doors were not. We had been sharing the cell for about a week and I quickly became aware that he was an erratic drug addict and his mood very unpredictable. As I was the older inmate in the cell, I had the bottom bunk and he was on the top. One late afternoon, I came into the cell not realising that he was asleep in the top bunk and opened the curtains and back window to let some fresh air in. The sunlight immediately woke him and he flew into a vicious rage. I apologised profusely and explained that I was not aware that he was there and asleep. I quickly closed the curtains again and he went back to sleep.

    I can't recall whether it was that night or the next when I was in bed and suddenly woke up struggling for breath. I felt an enormous weight on my chest and, as I had been fast asleep, it took me a couple of seconds to become aware of what was happening. I tried to move, but found myself pinned to the bed. As my eyes adjusted to the darkness of the room, I looked up and my cellmate was sitting on top of me, his legs immobilising my arms and his full weight on my chest. To my horror, I now also felt his hand on my throat and realised that he was completely naked. His hand was choking me, making it impossible for me to call out for help and I was too out-muscled to push him off. I was desperately trying to wriggle out from under his weight but I was trapped and powerless. Gasping for air, my mouth opened and in that instant he thrust his penis all the way to the back of my throat. I was now overcome with terror. I could barely breathe, was starting to feel very lightheaded and desperately hoping that I would not black out. I was petrified that should I pass out, I might not wake again. He was now verbally berating me in a combination of English and his native tongue, while continuing to force his penis further down my throat.

I am unsure exactly how long I was pinned to the bed, or why he stopped, but he suddenly jumped off me and repeatedly shouted that I should never cross him again. At almost the same instant, one of the other inmates came charging through the door and threw the guy out of my cell. To this day, I do not know how he knew the predicament I was in, but very few things in jail go unnoticed.

I did not leave my cell the next day at all and had no idea what would happen when he was to return to the cell the following night. When it came time for the evening muster the following night and we had to stand outside our cell, I was sick to my stomach in anticipation. When he stood next to me and as we turned to go into the cell, I noticed that he had a fresh and nasty black eye. From that moment, I was reasonably confident that he would not touch or talk to me again. A couple of days later, he was moved to another jail.

No inmate or officer ever spoke to me about the incident. It was as if it had never happened. I am, however, sure that someone had my back that night and take comfort in that it could have been so much worse. It took me years to speak to anyone about what happened and only then did I begin to understand the long-term impact of internalising the incident.

Tyre Kickers

In 1998, as a major shareholder, I came into a large sum of money when my employer, the retailer Specialty Fashion Group (SFG), listed on the ASX. Looking to minimise the tax liability of the windfall, I spent the next few months meeting with a number of financial advisors, but nothing really appealed. When I eventually connected with my accountant at the time, he enthusiastically told me about a particular tax loophole that could allow me to invest in a certain class of start-up business and as such negate any tax liability on the sale of my shares in SFG. The idea of investing in a new business and having a substantial stake was incredibly appealing. My accountant therefore suggested that I meet with one of his trusted business associates, Richard Bamford, who had laid the groundwork for an exciting start-up venture. The meeting was subsequently quickly set up in Double Bay in Sydney's eastern suburbs.

Richard was a very affable and appeared to be a successful corporate executive turned entrepreneur. He presented a detailed business plan of his latest venture and, from then on, courted my investment. He described his business idea as a revolutionary and innovative sustainability start-up which involved creating Australia's largest tyre recycling plant with the capability of manufacturing a number of products from the recycled material. The idea of a green start-up was appealing to me on a number of levels, including my belief that environmentally focused businesses were the way of the future.

Richard also told me that he was making good headway with securing other sophisticated investors interested in providing capital to the venture. I asked many questions and tried to adhere to the same protocols that I would advise friends and colleagues to follow when exploring new business opportunities. Foolishly, however, I did not do the due diligence on the legitimacy of some of the other investors, nor did I explore my own accountant's motives for the introduction. We had been professionally associated for some time and I thought I knew him well. I examined the financials and business plan and showed it to some business confidants. Based on the material that I had presented, everyone seemed excited at this unique and interesting opportunity. I sat with the information for about a week and then organised a second meeting.

During the week, I met with my accountant again and we agreed on the amount that I would invest in this new venture. It was now the early 2000s and my investment was agreed to be $500,000, an amount that, according to projections, would take a few years to burn through without the need for further capital. My contribution was to be structured as a loan to the new venture and paid back over twenty-four months.

Once my investment was made, the wheels turned very quickly on getting the new venture operational. Equipment was ordered from overseas, staff were recruited, potential sales agents were being sourced nationally and a large warehouse was leased. I was fired up by the excitement and speed of the set-up. That said, I was only able to be involved at an arm's length as my nine-to-five job took up most of my time.

Some months later, I was told that the funding from the other investors had not materialised and we were burning through the funds at our disposal faster than projected. Despite securing some great sales, we were fighting with local council and the EPA to allow the recycling of tyres and the mass storage of crumb rubber. This presented a delay in production and getting the new venture fully operational and also put a strain on our cash. The only income-producing activity the business was able to undertake was to store and aggregate used tyres. In essence, this meant that rather than companies dumping used tyres themselves and paying a fee as required in NSW, we were able to do it on their behalf for a lesser fee. We would then turn the tyres into crumbed rubber and remove all the steel casings.

While we were seeking additional funding via traditional banking and private investment, I extended the mortgage on my house to free up cash for the business and obtained a larger equity stake. Looking back, however, this enabled further expansion of the business and, during that time, the opportunity to purchase the building that housed the business also presented itself. The mortgage repayments were only marginally more than the rent that the business was paying and hence the move made good sense, especially as I was convinced in the viability of this venture.

The excitement of the new property acquisition, however, was a short-lived honeymoon. The reality that the venture was quickly running out of cash once more became apparent. In the limited time I had to focus on the business, I was preoccupied with sales and growth and left all operational responsibilities to Richard, the appointed CEO.

Richard and I were soon meeting more regularly, as what should have been weekly business catch-ups quickly became cash crisis discussions. At one of them, Richard told me that he managed to secure the sale of a twenty-five per cent stake in the business, which would not only provide much needed capital, but also allow the pay down of some of my loans to the venture. And so, after a very expensive due diligence process, the sale was proposed to happen two weeks after both parties had agreed. The terms of the deal included a partial payment on the day of settlement, with the full balance being split into three monthly payments thereafter.

On the day of settlement, the first payment was made and quickly deposited towards the property mortgage and outstanding staff wages. Unfortunately, however, this was to be the one and only time the business ever received funds from this deal. It soon came to light that our new business partners were under investigation by federal agencies and had all their assets frozen. In the end, the contracts were rescinded and we found ourselves back to our cash-poor reality.

Choices

Around the time we found ourselves without the promised seed investor, a substantial invoice for electrical work for our venture came to me for approval. All supplier expenses were co-signed with Richard and therefore it was not unusual for me to quickly tend to these invoices while at my full-time work.

In the case of this particular invoice, the supplier's name was familiar to me as they had contracted to SFG previously. All store-related expenses were my responsibility and approving invoices was a daily task. SFG had an annual turnover of hundreds of millions of dollars. Therefore, an invoice of this size was common and quickly paid without question.

And just like that, it happened that I approved and sent the invoice incurred for electrical work by our venture for payment to the accounts department of my employer, SFG. It was only when Richard told me that the supplier had called to express gratitude at our prompt and full payment, that I realised my mistake.

I would love to say something redeeming and insightful at this point, but the reality is that when I realised that the payment had been made due to my error, I was initially conflicted as to how to immediately rectify the situation. I was becoming increasingly anxious over the venture and the short-term cash holiday that this could afford was tempting. Nonetheless, I suggested to Richard that we should meet to work out a plan to repay the money. When we met, Richard told me that the funds had already been used to cover other company expenses.

Accepting that there were no immediate funds to pay my employer back, I decided to do nothing for the time being. A black mark against what was otherwise a clean record, I told myself. And I was sure that I would work it out. Richard meanwhile couldn't resist the light-hearted jibes about my financial infidelity and suddenly having a funding alternative, should things further deteriorate with our business.

A few weeks later, Richard handed me another invoice for co-approval and made it abundantly clear that there weren't sufficient funds to cover the outstanding amount. Noting that it needed to be urgently paid, he suggested that I take care of this one, like the last one, as well. My first reaction was a definitive no, prompting a series of tough and heated meetings over the ensuing days. I was reminded of the reality that the business was close to folding and the fact that if we let it unravel now, we would lose everything, including my house. We strategised extensively about the short and medium-term opportunities and fast tracking them as much as possible. I was repeatedly assured that the business just needed a bit more time to be fully up and running. And a few days later, I submitted the second fraudulent invoice to SFG for payment.

At that point, and in fact all along, my intention was to repay the funds in total and I believed that Richard was on the same page too. We figured that once the business was generating income or, more likely, we reignited the capital raising, we would be in a position to repay the debt. After knowingly submitting the second invoice, I was sure that I would be falling on the sword at some stage in the future and that there would be very serious consequences for my actions. My naïve thinking, however, was that if I had the money to settle the debt and admitted impropriety before being found out, I might be lucky and avoid criminal repercussions, which could prove embarrassing for SFG, being a publicly listed company.

Keep On Digging

Over the next few months, I approved a further six or seven invoices for payment, initially for a few hundred dollars each that over time blew out to elaborate invoices for full shop reconstructions. The fraudulent invoices would be triggered by a specific amount that Richard would strongly advise that our business needed. The pattern of invoicing was to create one invoice at a time that was aligned with the weekly automated payment schedule within our finance department.

Around this time, Richard also informed me that he had set up a number of shelf companies should we ever need invoices created and paid to assist the business. He often hinted at the trouble that I would be in if my fraudulent activities were uncovered, especially ahead of our capacity to pay it all back. Perversely, as Richard spoke of the shelf companies, I thought that it would enable me to fill some of the holes that had been dug with the other invoices and, of course, buy us more time.

Richard and I consulted weekly in person or on the phone for financial updates. He was the CEO during the entire time and my only source of information. The roller coaster of one step forward and two steps back, however, meant that there were many weeks without any financial pressure and need for more funding. During that time, the conversations were highly optimistic around new contracts and opportunities paving the way for the business to turn the corner. Other weeks, additional funds were imperative to keep the business afloat and see it come to fruition.

When we talked about the exit strategy and the plan to refund the money to SFG, Richard and I estimated that with the contracts under negotiation coming into effect, combined with plant, equipment and a realistic PE, the business would be valued at over twenty-five million.

Every time I reflect on this vicious cycle now, I am taken back to the shame, guilt and fear that would overcome me every night an invoice was fraudulently created. Each time, I wondered if it would be when I was caught. But over the years and as the pattern and associated feelings became more and more familiar, I developed an overarching sense of detachment from the world as well as my physical and spiritual self. I still can't grasp that it went on for four years. But I guess time flies when you are lost at sea and land is nowhere to be seen.

And while I make no excuses for my crime, my life was incredibly busy during those years. I had a job managing a portfolio of at least a thousand leases and was focused on expanding our portfolio. I worked long hours and travelled every week and also had a young family with three children under ten.

During the first year of the venture, I remember constantly toying with the decision to cut all losses, possibly folding the business, losing my house and facing the consequences. To say I wish I had would be way too trite. Having spent the last decade unpacking what happened and who I am, I have an understanding of how easily things can get out of control. However, I struggle to reconcile with the part of me that went down the wrong path.

And to this day, I believe that the venture was ahead of its time and, given correct funding and management, it would have been a success despite the early setbacks.

King Richard

Richard and I never socialised and rarely ran into each other socially. Ours was a purely professional relationship, where two people were equally vested in the same successful outcome, despite the wrongdoings that we were co-conspirators in.

For the entire duration of our business partnership, I was under the impression that both Richard and his wife Patricia, who not only acted as a receptionist at his office but was also his part-time bookkeeper, had multiple sources of income from other business activities to maintain their privileged lifestyle and multiple stylish offices.

Until of course, as I later found out with a crashing thud, he maintained his five-star lifestyle with his director's fee and imaginative use of company capital. Creatively packaged into the monthly accounts were extensive capital equipment acquisitions, which later turned out to be personal art, jewellery, furniture and other lifestyle luxuries and, much later on, the purchase of a boat.

The reality of my own business partner using the venture's cash for his private gain would only come to light when I found myself sitting in a courtroom with Richard during the civil proceedings. Richard and I last communicated the afternoon of the first court summons, the day after I was confronted and terminated at work. Upon my suggestion, we met in the waiting area outside the courtroom, at which time I found out that, while I was being fired, Richard was being served papers to appear in court.

To my astonishment, the encounter was brutal and brief, with Richard simply saying, "That's it, mate. We're fucked. You're on your own." He walked away and those were the last words we ever spoke.

We both engaged separate counsel and for the rest of the civil proceedings, would only see each other in court, our case being co-joined as directors of the business. Richard had decided that he would not disclose his correct and true financial position as directed by the courts. On the day the judge called for him to stand in the dock to be cross-examined about his financial affairs, Richard was nowhere to be found. While it may have surprised some in the courtroom, I totally expected it to happen. In what must have been a well-planned escape, Richard and his wife fled the country the night before. Under the nose of the court, over the previous few days and later well documented in most newspapers, they had managed to dispose of much of their highly valued assets, including cars, boat, furniture and extensive artwork, and presumably left the country cashed up for a life on the run.

I didn't know many of their friends and they had no children or family I had ever met. The only Australian connection I knew of by name was a well-known Australian designer whose son they were the godparents of. As widely reported and confirmed by the authorities, the two left on Japan Airlines bound for Tokyo, never to be seen again. To this day, an international arrest warrant stands should they ever be located in a country of extradition to Australia, assuming that they are still alive or not incarcerated elsewhere for another crime.

Having lost my father at the age of ten years old and being mostly raised by my maternal grandfather, I now realise that I had a tendency, primarily in business, to build strong mentor-style associations with more mature and seemingly accomplished men. Richard fell into that category, particularly as he did not have children of his own. Early on in the piece, he treated me in a paternal manner and I let my guard down and trusted him almost implicitly. In hindsight, I feel very foolish, because I really walked straight into the situation and acted quite out of character in so willingly surrendering my trust.

WTF

I will always struggle with understanding how I embezzled that quantity of money and the sheer number of invoices involved. When I was caught and found out the amount, I was totally gobsmacked. Had I been told the amount was five to six million, it would likely have been the number that had been floating in my mind and therefore would not have been a great surprise. However, when I was told that the amount was in excess of sixteen million, it truly was my WTF moment. At no point did I think that we had amassed that amount and I was absolutely astonished.

Another surprising revelation was when Charles Waterstreet told me that, once the fraud was in excess of a few million dollars, the rest was academic and the total amount did not really matter. I learnt through the course of the criminal proceedings that, although my conviction was a forgone conclusion, my legal team and the DPP were in effect 'horse trading' over the specific charges that I would plead guilty to. The negotiations ultimately rendered the exact amount that I was charged with redundant, which was yet another WTF moment for me.

To this day, I can't be sure whether the amount I embezzled is accurate and correct or what accounting practices led to the amount. Despite being presented with about thirty legal boxes of documents, I simply did not have the emotional capacity to cross-reference the financials provided. Besides, to do so would not have helped my case whatsoever or have impacted my ultimate sentencing. This again was made abundantly clear to me by Charles Waterstreet and his team and therefore I made peace with the amount, even though its accuracy will forever be an unknown to me.

As if the magnitude of my wrongdoing wasn't enough to face, the insistent portrayal by the media of me being a greedy mastermind that surely syphoned the funds offshore was most certainly another WTF-have-I-done realisation.

A Fortunate Boy

The first nine years of my life was a very typical Australian dream. Two loving parents, a younger sister and a happy life in the 1970s in suburban Perth. We lived a very comfortable middle-class existence and our life revolved around the ocean and sports. I went to a very small Jewish school and my entire year consisted of twenty other kids. Fortunately, as my first passion growing up was swimming and I was part of a large swim squad and a separate swim club, there were plenty of opportunities to expand my circle of friends. Life in Perth in the 70s meant jumping on your Malvern Star bike to visit friends and hang until sunset. I was lucky that all my mother's family and most of my father's family also resided in Perth. Grandparents, uncles, aunties and cousins aplenty.

Some of my fondest family memories were sitting on my maternal grandfather's lap, formerly Uri Eisenstadt and now Ken Steele, watching English soccer or VFL games, as they were known back then, while he had a Scotch in one hand and a cigarette in the other. I will never forget Christmas Day in 1974 when my entire family crowded around my grandparents' TV to watch the first-ever colour transmission of the annual Christmas parade. It was probably the first time I became aware that we had more than the average family, as we were one of the first in Perth with a colour TV. Naturally, as a child I did not understand that it was my grandparents' wealth that allowed their travel for extended periods and their ownership of lovely homes here and back in Israel.

My father, David, was a very talented athlete and worked as an engineer for the state government. He followed in the footsteps of his father, my paternal grandfather, Simon Ferdinand Feldman, whom I was named after. Oddly, the tradition in Jewish families is to not name newborns after living relatives. However, my grandfather was known and referred to since childhood as Ferdie Feldman. Most people did not even connect him with his real name of Simon. And therefore, it was acceptable to name me after him.

Many years later, I discovered that Ferdie, as a talented university rugby student had represented the university team in a match against the New Zealand All Blacks. It was such an odd late-life revelation, as, growing up in Perth, I did not even know that rugby union or rugby league existed. My father's family were diehard Australian Rules football followers. My father even played Colts (reserve grade) for East Perth, the team my family followed for many years.

In the mid-70s, my parents, with the financial backing of my maternal grandfather, took the opportunity to reinvent themselves as furniture retailers. They pioneered the Scandinavian modular style of furniture and home décor. It was a hugely successful venture and the name of the store was Kings Paddington. In homage to the Scandinavian flavour, we even bought a Volvo as our family car and life was good.

Around 1976, my father started to suffer from increasingly frequent headaches. As children, my younger sister and I were shielded from anything that was not happy and pleasant. At the end of 1976, however, we found out that my father had an inoperable brain tumour. As a last resort, before chemo and radiotherapy were due to start, my mother, father, sister and I travelled to San Francisco to stay with my uncle in an attempt to investigate any new forms of treatment. It was our first and only overseas trip as a family.

When we returned from the US, my father started a very aggressive course of cancer treatment and, as a result of the cortisone included, he ballooned to more than double his size and lost all his hair. I never came to terms with the transformation of the fittest person I knew, especially as neither of my parents ever drank or smoked. My father literally grew to a mass of a human incapable of doing much other than sit and stare. My sister and I did not know what to do when this new version of our father came to watch our sport or pick us up with my mother from school. While we were protected from most of what was going on, the physical reality was too obvious to hide.

Towards the end of 1977, my father's health was at its worst and he was hospitalised. My grandfather and mother decided that for my father's last months of life, his children should be taken overseas. The last time I saw my father was when my mother took my sister and me into his hospital room to say goodbye before we flew overseas. Even as a young boy, I knew it would be the last time that I would see my father, a reality that was not spoken of.

I will never forget walking into my father's hospital room and not recognising the person who lay there. We hadn't been allowed to see him for the previous month and by now he had wasted away and presented as a grey, sleeping shell of a man hardly resembling the man he once was. To this day, the moment I walk into a hospital, I can smell his room. To me, it is the smell of death. My father sadly was not in a state to say goodbye to us as he was largely in and out of consciousness. My sister and I stood and hovered over him for what seemed like ages and then we were shuffled out. Miraculously, as I would later find out, despite the condition he was in, he garnered the strength to leave his hospital room some days later, stole a bicycle and rode to his best friend's house to say goodbye and then went back to his hospital bed.

Israel

My sister, Nikki, and I found ourselves with my maternal grandparents on a plane to Israel a few days after our last hospital visit. For a ten-year-old boy and an eight-year-old girl, suddenly finding yourself in a strange country, listening to a native language you barely understand and meeting and visiting family we did not know was overwhelming. We were hosted by our extended family, who went to great lengths to take my sister and me to all the historic and biblical landmarks of Israel and to make our stay as memorable and no doubt distracting as possible. I remember that part of our trip as being full of adventure, laughter and new experiences. The richness of Israel was an incredible experience for two kids from Perth. Every afternoon, we would get a phone call from my mother back in Perth saying hi and naturally I would always ask after Dad. My question was generally met with 'He's OK,' followed by a rapid change of subject.

Perhaps a month into our stay in Israel, we received the call. I clearly remember my grandfather talking to my mother, taking his glasses off and sitting down with his head in his hands, then turning to my sister and me. He put down the phone without us speaking to our mother, walked over to Nikki and me, sat down next to us and very lovingly told us that our dad was gone, he had passed away. The room was silent and I distinctly recall looking from my grandfather's face to my grandmother's and then my sister's, and then I went into a bedroom to curl up underneath a bed. Although I do not remember how long I was there for, I was told years later that it was many hours.

We did not speak to our mother for some days after the phone call. While that might seem very odd and certainly mystified me for many years, I learnt later that the reason was to shield the young from trauma and therefore not uncommon. In fact, one of my most vivid memories from that time was when the day after my father's death, Nikki and I were taken to a party to watch the *Wizard of Oz* with a group of kids we did not know. To this day, I get teary everytime I see that movie.

We spent another month after my father's passing in Israel, my grandparents doing everything they could to make life as normal as possible. They even sent us to a local school for a week as a bit of an adventure.

Oddly enough, I do not recall leaving Israel, despite the fact that so many things that happened during that trip still feel so real. Our return to Perth is, however, a total blank. I do not even recall the first time I saw my mother again.

From the time we returned to Perth, I felt that my mother had changed from her normal and affectionate self to being quite distant and at times cold. I can't imagine what it would be like to suddenly find yourself a single mother of two at thirty-four years, especially after losing the man she had been with since she was fifteen years old. It would be some twenty years later before my mother would speak about my father openly to me and that would only be if I asked questions. Not being able to attend my father's funeral has been a constant pain that I have carried to this day. It wasn't until my twenties, over ten years after my father's death, that I had the courage to visit his grave.

Almost immediately upon arrival back in Perth, life returned to normal and I went back to school. About nine months later, my mother told my sister and me that it was time for a change and that the two of us would go and live in San Francisco with my late father's brother and family to attend school and have another adventure. During that time, my mother and a friend of hers, also recently widowed, would take an extended holiday and travel around the USA together. She assured us that she would visit of course.

School in the US sounded incredibly exciting for an eleven-year-old and the thought of catching the yellow bus, just like the movies, to school every day seemed like a cool adventure. Further, my uncle had three boys and the idea of acquiring three brothers was equally appealing. Based on my memories of our previous visit to the US, the opportunity of living on campus added to the adventure. My aunt and uncle were professors at Stanford University and resided on campus as most academics in the US do.

I recall all my Perth mates treating me like some rock star because I was going to live in the US. My popularity soared as it all sounded so glamorous to the outside world. Nikki and I, however, were still reeling from our whirlwind trip to Israel, the death of our father and trying to fit into our old lives back in Perth without him.

Life in San Francisco

Within the first few days of our arrival to the south of San Francisco, my mother started her travels around the US and we stayed in my aunt and uncle's care, living in their home at Stanford.

On my first day at Lucille M. Nixon Elementary School in the sixth grade, I felt like a celebrity. Coming from Australia and having an Australian accent was the novelty of all novelties at that time. The incredible pride and patriotism that young American schoolkids had for their country struck me first, evidenced by everyone standing to sing the national anthem and reciting the Pledge of Allegiance at the start of every morning. I'm pretty sure that I was able to recite the pledge before I even knew all the verses of 'Advance Australia Fair'. I was surprised to see that public schools in the US did not have uniforms and, unlike Australia, meals were served to all kids in a cafeteria and the meal plan was pretty much one size fitted all.

As the newbies, my sister and I were conscious and intimidated by the fashion line-up at the school. We certainly did not want to be attracting the wrong attention for our less than cool Down Under attire. The trend at the time was fancy designer jeans and everyone was looking to out dress the other. Needless to say, our Lee and Levi jeans, albeit very designer in Australia, were pretty much bargain basement to our new friends. Another fad that had not yet arrived in Australia was the glam rock big hairstyle well worn by Charlie's Angels, Chips and Magnum P.I. I arrived with a magnificently coiffed bowl haircut and my Dunlop Volleys. My accent and my first pair of Adidas Romes, however, saved the day.

Most of the socialising happened on the famous yellow school bus to and from school every day. The pupils at my school were a mix of children of academics, doctors and kids from wealthy families in the surrounding hills. One my first buddies' father was a director at the National Geographic, which at the time was at the peak of its popularity. My first visit to his house in the hills was like walking into a hunter's lodge in the mid-west, which was quite confronting and by today's standards completely non-PC. Almost every wall featured a stuffed animal's head and all floors and furniture were covered in animal skin and fur. Amazing photographs and paintings lined the walls.

When my sister and I went shopping with my aunt and uncle at the local campus mall, we expected just a handful of shops, given that it was a university campus. We could not believe our eyes, however, driving into what was actually an American mega mall right in the middle of the Stanford University grounds. Who would have thought that we would find a few department stores, supermarkets and around sixty speciality shops. In fact, this campus mall housed the first ever Bloomingdales that operated outside of New York. Equally impressive to me was the local ice creamery, which had up to forty flavours.

Back at the family house, my aunt and uncle, suddenly caring for five kids on a limited academic income, were understandably frugal. To this day, I eat with lightning speed so that I do not miss out and I find it difficult to have any leftovers go to waste. I shared a room with my cousin closest in age to me and my sister shared with the younger twin boys. It was a very respectful and intellectual household while at the same time absolutely, and thankfully, sport obsessed. Friday night was game night. We would watch the 49ers during the NFL season and the Giants in the MLB season.

My aunt and uncle became my surrogate parents very quickly. They were loving and nurturing, and treated us as their own. There was very little fighting among the five kids and we quickly developed a close bond, especially me, who now had an accomplice for every sport and physical activity. To enable my sister and me with some familiar activities resembling Perth life, we joined the local swim team and we forged friendships that still exist today. Overall, I believe that the new-found family dynamic in San Francisco helped fill some of the void that my father's death had left.

Whenever my mum would return to see us, she would stay at the local motel called the Tiki Inn. She generally only stayed for a few days at a time and, for some reason,

I was actually excited when she would leave. On one of her visits, she took my sister and I to see snow for the very first time. I remember driving through Reno and into Lake Tahoe and seeing snow. It was pure magic. As you can imagine, coming from Perth where one barely needs a jacket in winter, the cold was quite a novelty. As was seeing fluorescent all-in-one ski jumpsuits and reflector glasses everywhere.

Each time my mother visited us, we would take a few days and have an adventure with her. We went to theme parks, the city, countryside and beach holidays and occasionally my aunt, uncle and cousins would join us. One such trip that sticks in my mind is a beach holiday to the dunes south of San Jose. We rode around in dune buggies and spent the day in the water looking for sea treasures. At the end of this trip, I clearly remember thinking that this was what family should be all about.

My school, no doubt based on my accent, asked if I would play the lead role in the year-end Shakespeare play, *The Taming of the Shrew*. This was my first-ever performance on stage and was where I discovered that I had no problem with performing in public. Recognising that, my family enrolled me in the local amateur theatre and I performed in a couple of productions, which I imagine also served as an escape. The fantasy world that the productions created was my personal Disneyland.

As an Australian in an American elementary school in the Bay area, I will never forget my first earthquake. It was a normal school day and as we finished off our morning recital of 'The Star-Spangled Banner', the classroom started to shake and, like a well-oiled machine, the teachers and students almost innately jumped under their desks and I quickly followed suit. The picture that is stamped in my mind is that, because the teacher was unable to jump under her desk, she stood in the door frame. It had never occurred to me, until I was told later, that most structures in the Bay area were designed and built with door frames that were the strongest and safest point in an earthquake. The earthquake only lasted a few minutes, although it felt much longer, and when it was over, everyone resumed their activities as if nothing had happened. In the scheme of earthquakes in San Francisco, it was a mild tremor and nothing on the scale of the many destructive ones that the area is known for.

As one of the top universities in the US, Stanford University campus is famous for many things. One of the features on the campus grounds was the proliferation of Rodin statues. Every walking, reading or relaxation area on campus featured Rodin's work. On subsequent visits to Stanford as a young man, I would spend time in these quiet spaces, as they were a soothing place for me. To this day, I still have a craving for the tranquillity that the gardens provided.

On the opposite end of the spectrum of memorable places was my first of numerous visits to Alcatraz. As a young boy, I recall being completely overwhelmed by the cold and eerie confines of the jail. The basic structure of rock, metal and concrete made me wonder how anyone could have actually survived there. On my first visit, we joined a guided tour highlighting the harsh life that inmates faced in the facility and also found out about some of its famous former residents. When the tour stopped outside a jail cell that had been kept in original condition, the guide called for a volunteer to step forward to experience being locked in a cell. I put my hand up and, upon being selected, was asked to step into the cell and the guide locked the barred door behind me. The cell offered no privacy and I could see the rest of the group, as well as every cell in that area. While I stood in the locked cell, the tour guide explained about the meals, clothing and bedding that was given to inmates. I remember it being a warm San Francisco day, but the cell, with no heating or cooling, was like an icebox. The bed was steel mesh with a thin mattress and the toilet was built into the cell. Despite my mock lock-up lasting only a few minutes, I remember being frightened and claustrophobic. When the tour group was led out to the yard where inmates would have spent their recreation time, there was no grass, just a couple of basketball courts surrounded by concrete stands.

The Bay where Alcatraz is located is renowned for its heavy fog, currents and cold winds. Again, despite it being a sunny day, the cold wind ripped through the yard. When we eventually left the prison by boat, I thought about the men the tour guide spoke of who had escaped and whose bodies were never found. I couldn't imagine anyone surviving in that water. Years later, when I was faced with the inevitability of jail, my mind immediately jumped to images of Alcatraz and the fear that all jails were just like that quickly set in.

Of all the places in the world that I have lived and travelled to, San Francisco continues to have the most powerful hold over me. I was sad when it was time to return to Perth many months later and I was also filled with angst and trepidation. The thought of going to back to our old family home without my father was very daunting.

Back in Perth

Back in Australia, our life in Perth returned to relative normality quite fast, with school, sport, family and friends in full swing. Although I had always been close to my maternal grandfather, his presence and influence after my father's death was even more prevalent. Our connection was no longer just sitting on his lap during visits. After my return from the US, I quickly became his shadow and as he had three daughters, he treated me like a son. My sister and I would spend at least a couple of nights a week with my grandparents. My grandfather would talk to me about business, world affairs and sport, and there was always some connection to our Eastern European Jewish heritage. Our relationship was probably quite mature for my age, but even so I would listen to all he had to say with great interest.

Every Saturday, my grandfather would take me to Hay Street Mall in the city, where Katies' head office was. Back in those days, garments were often made, or at least finished, locally. Upstairs from the main Katies store was a small garment factory with seamstresses and tailors furiously working away on old Singer sewing machines, often with cigarette in mouth. Every one of the ladies knew me by name and it was there that I learnt the reverence with which my grandfather was held. At that time and even as an adult, when we walked down Hay Street Mall or walked into a Perth restaurant, my grandfather would be treated as royalty.

On many occasions in Perth, I would enter a store or café alone and, if the owner realised who my grandfather was, I too would get favourable treatment. I quickly came to realise that my grandfather was pretty universally regarded as a true European old-school gentleman. He was admired for being a successful businessman who made everyone around him feel important and valued. I never heard my grandfather raise his voice or speak ill of others. However, what he wanted to get done usually happened to plan and without conflict.

My grandfather also had an innate ability to present himself, even the way he dressed, in a subtle, classy and dignified way. He pioneered black sneakers with dress pants and shirt long before anyone else. A couple of anecdotes that I still carry with me today include, "Every minute you are late is ten minutes less respect you have for the person" and he would always tell me that whenever he would do a business deal, all parties had to walk away as winners otherwise it was not a deal. This was a stark contrast to the cute anecdote that he would tell me every Friday night: "We were so poor during the war that the only time we would buy chicken was if we were sick or the chicken was sick."

Having a larger-than-life grandfather so firmly perched on a pedestal by our community gave me a sense of identity and presence as a child. I was forever focused on making him proud. His validation was incredibly important to me and he never stopped being my idol and superhero. I would say that this dynamic was a guiding force through my life and my desire to be like him at all costs was a pretty unstoppable force.

Looking back now, I have a lot more clarity on how my blind adulation for my grandfather was as unhealthy for me as it was inspiring. Perhaps the European cultural curse of a dominant patriarch creates unrealistic expectations on the younger generations and does not provide enough room for individual growth and the formation of one's identity. To this day, however, I still use his phrases and expressions. Of course, I often wonder how he would have reacted to my downfall. Equally, I wonder how he would view my journey since then.

My grandfather came from a very wealthy family in Poland who lost everything during World War II. He would always remind me that everything can change overnight and one should always make the most of today. In jail, I often thought about the truth of that statement, having had so much and then losing it all. The most painful reflections about my grandfather in jail centred on the dignity that he never lost. I, however, of my own doing, ended up in a system designed to break you, one where dignity was second to survival.

Move to Sydney

About six months after my sister, mother and I returned from the US, my mother announced that we would be selling our house, packing up and moving to Sydney, making it our fourth new city in two years. The move to Sydney was more daunting than Israel or the US, probably because we did not have any family or connections there. The process of selling our house, packing all our belongings and saying farewell to friends and family felt final and gut-wrenching, despite the fact that we returned to Perth many times each year to visit and always stayed with my grandparents. The finality of our move set in when my sister and I were sitting on the front lawn of our home, next to the sold sign, watching our family Volvo being loaded on a truck en route to Sydney.

Our first night in Sydney, my mum took us for dinner to the famous Gelato Bar at Bondi Beach, as she had heard that the matzo dumpling soup would make us all feel right at home. I vividly recall walking along Bondi Beach's Campbell Parade for the very first time, which in the early 1980s was buzzing with people well into the night. It was totally eye opening for my sister and me, as we were used to a sleepy small-town setting. I was very happy to find out that the matzo dumpling soup was incredible and so was the apple strudel we had for dessert.

Our first home in Sydney was in Bondi's Penkivil Street, the heart of the Orthodox Jewish community. It was a three-bedroom apartment in a quiet block which took us a while to get used to, given that we were used to an abundance of indoor and outdoor space in Perth. The building we lived in had a shared swimming pool, which we thought was only the case in hotels. We quickly made friends with most of the young families in the building and soon discovered that many of our new friends were already attending the school that we were enrolled in.

Soon after our arrival, my mum started a job as a travel agent, which was a boom industry in the 1980s. My sister and I joined the local swim club, again to take on activities familiar to us. Not long after our move, I found myself babysitting my sister regularly as my mother started dating again. We hardly ever met her suitors. However, she would from time to time tell us if she met someone she liked. Ironically enough, one of those suitors was a well-known judge with whom I would cross paths many years later as inmates in the same jail.

My new school in Sydney seemed absolutely enormous to me. Coming from an entire grade of around eighteen kids to a school that had at least three classes of twenty-five children in each grade was socially confronting. The first time I went to the school tuck shop was like walking into a party. Unlike the structured canteen in the US or the absence of one in Perth, this was a large window to treat heaven. I am sure that the tuck shop at today's Moriah College is equipped with a broader range of dietary requirements, not to mention many five-star health options and bento boxes aplenty.

On my very first day in class, the weather was hot and humid. About twenty minutes into the first lesson, our teacher asked someone to open the back window to let some air in. One of boys went to the back window and, as he was trying to push it open, his hand went straight through the plate glass, badly cutting his hand. The wound was bleeding profusely and the kid looked a bit shocked. The teacher turned to me and asked me to take him to the school nurse. Of course, I had no idea where to go, but did not want to look foolish and draw any attention. So we walked into the hallway together and the injured boy turned to me and said, "You have no idea where to go, do you?" When I nodded and told him no, he shrugged and said, "I'll take you." And that was the start of my friendship with one of my best friends to this day. Forty-three years later, he still has the scar on his hand.

I quickly gravitated to the sportier kids who seemed to have the run of the playground. One of the more colourful characters of the school was the janitor, who would take us into the janitor's room and share his collection of girlie magazines with us. Our visits were always very clandestine and quick of course, but we did get to enjoy a wide range of material courtesy of Hugh Hefner and Larry Flynt, unfortunately not included in the school's sex education curriculum.

Not long into my first year, I was playing touch football with a group of boys on the concrete basketball court. One of them fell and ripped his leg open on the chain wire fence, a scar he also bares to this day. That incident marked the beginning of my lifelong friendship with another one of my closest friends. Two of my biggest supporters and confidants through thick and thin literally came into my life by accident.

I struggled with the strong emphasis on academia at my school and after two years, at the end of year nine, it was time to move on or, more accurately, I was asked to not come back to the school. I guess my commitment to entertaining my classmates was not appreciated by the teaching faculty and I was deemed not suited to Moriah College.

By that time, my mother had met a partner who later became her husband and we relocated to the leafy North Shore as she set up house with my future stepfather. I was sent to Killara High School, which ended up being the right fit for me.

Mr Steele Abroad

Our new life on Sydney's North Shore following my mother's marriage was very comfortable. In addition to gaining three stepsisters, we lived in a big house and wanted for nothing. All five children got on very well and grew even closer during the ensuing years, despite often being separated by geography.

There is no doubt that despite the distance between my grandfather and me, we grew even closer over the coming years. Looking back, I can see that he was preparing me to follow him into a career in the rag trade. I still marvel at the fact that in his seventies, my grandfather started a new retail business that eventually became an iconic Western Australian institution.

One of the most meaningful events of my childhood was when, as a thirteen-year-old, my grandfather organised for my bar mitzvah to take place in Israel. No expense was spared in flying my sister, Mum and myself over. We all flew Alitalia in the days when smoking was permitted on board and I have a clear memory of the beautiful Italian hostesses smoking in the galley while on their break.

It was our second trip to Israel and the mood was entirely different to our first. Whereas the first trip was about losing my father, this trip was celebrating my becoming a man. One of the most symbolic parts of a bar mitzvah is standing with your father on the bimah, the prayer altar. For me, that part of the ceremony involved my grandfather assuming the role of my father.

My bar mitzvah celebrations further showcased the respect that existed towards Ken Steele, even a world away from Perth. At the luncheon following the service at the Western Wailing Wall, the room was not only filled with family and friends, but also included high-profile local business identities, lord mayors and other social figureheads. I was in awe of the esteem that he seemed to be held in and remember thinking that I absolutely wanted to be like him.

During our stay in Israel, my grandfather and I spent a lot of time walking the streets of Tel Aviv and Jerusalem and soaking up the local culture. People would call out to him often in several languages, be it Polish, Russian, Yiddish, Hebrew or English. I don't know why I never asked why so many people knew and obviously respected him. It was almost so natural that they did and he certainly took all the attention in his humble stride.

One of his foibles which he would explain was that as a survivor, he always wanted the security of somewhere to go, should he be forced to flee his country of primary residence. Hence, he thought it absolutely necessary to have an apartment in Israel as well. He also spoke of the importance to always look after family and told me about relatives of ours living in poverty in Russia, stuck and unable to leave the country. I learnt that during his stays in Israel he would send money to Russia, because oddly it was easier to do so from Israel than from Australia.

My trip to Israel was so meaningful that I really wanted to go back in later years to reconnect with the amazing memories and sensations that forever stayed with me after that visit. And so, when I was about seventeen-years-old, I returned alone with my best friend and retraced my visit as a thirteen-year-old, with my grandfather in the forefront of my mind.

Working-class Man

When I eventually finished school, my grandfather was quick to officially encourage me to follow a career path in retail. Suffice to say, I embraced it wholeheartedly, as I had no desire to go to university. Following his suggestion, I embarked on a retail traineeship with G.J.Coles, soon to be known as Coles Myer, and so for the next two years, I threw myself into learning everything possible about retail as a Kmart trainee manager. I naturally gravitated towards the apparel and soft furnishing divisions, although my friends still make fun of me for making daily red-light specials announcements on the store's PA system on such interesting items as toilet seats and flokati rugs.

While undertaking the traineeship, I was also studying a TAFE retail course at night or technical college as it was called back then.

The completion of the Kmart traineeship paved the way into a retail management job in a textile business affiliated with my grandfather's business interests. His business network namely spanned west coast to east coast and so the transition into a role in Sydney was easy.

Over the next seven years, I managed to gain experience across a wide range of roles within the retail and textile environment, culminating in opening my own small retail outlet in Sydney in 1994. Called Simon's Fashion Factory, the business was built around on-selling excess fashion merchandise. Each week, I would drive around fashion wholesalers that I had built relationships with and buy their overrun stock, selling it at my factory. My grandfather assisted with financing the fixtures and opening stock and the rest I was able to secure on trade credit. I was around twenty-seven years old and for the period that the factory was open, it supported me well.

About a year after I opened the store, two simultaneous events happened purely by fate. Firstly, I was approached by an emerging chain of ladies' fashion stores who wanted to purchase Simon's Fashion Factory and rebrand it to be theirs. I accepted their offer and sold the business. And then I was also fortuitously approached to buy into a consortium that wanted to roll out ladies' fashion stores nationally. At the time, the group had about half a dozen stores trading in NSW as Miller's Fashion Club.

My grandfather and I jointly invested in the new venture, funded by the sale of my business and also a loan by him. Business partners for the first time, my grandfather became the Western Australia partner and I the Queensland partner. At that point, my investment also required me to move to Queensland to set up the new venture.

Each state partner was tasked with opening as many stores as fast as possible in order to secure market share in the 'fashion for the masses' sector. Within a year and a half,

I opened eighteen stores in Queensland and it didn't take long for the overarching business to have a footprint of several hundred stores nationally.

At the end of the initial growth phase, I moved back to Sydney and spread myself across a national logistics role and a national property portfolio. The following four years were spent acquiring new businesses and brands, and preparing the business for the eventual ASX listing. Before listing in the late nineties, we consolidated all shareholdings into one holding company called Miller's Retail, soon to be renamed Specialty Fashion Group (SFG).

Post IPO, SFG quickly grew to a thousand stores, at which time I started to focus my time purely on the company's property portfolio. The early 2000s saw me travelling at least one or two days a week interstate as we were in full swing to optimise the company's profile. As my role within the company became more senior, particularly after the public listing, my grandfather sold his stake as he was now well into his eighties and decided to just focus on his textile business in WA.

It did not take long for SFG to claim the title of the largest female specialty retailer in Australia. I often sought advice and guidance from my grandfather in managing SFG's property portfolio. I relied on his insights and business acumen and truly enjoyed connecting with him outside the grandfather to grandson dynamic. Time and time again, landlords that I was dealing with knew of my grandfather, as his reputation truly preceded him.

One day I was renewing a lease for one of our stores which happened to be the first ever Katies that opened back in 1956. To my amazement, the landlord sent me the original lease documents dating back to the 1960s. I could not believe it when I noticed my grandfather's name as one of the lessee guarantors. There I was, some forty years later, negotiating on the exact same property. It was a real watershed moment.

The Circle of Life

As my business life evolved, I settled down and got married and started a family. My first daughter was born in 2000, followed by my second daughter in 2003 and a son in 2007. My mother truly relished being a grandmother and played a big part in both my daughters' early life. Despite my grandparents living in Perth, they made regular trips to the east coast to spend time with their great grandkids.

My elder daughter had her fifth birthday party in October 2005. My instinct that something was not right was triggered when my mum did not attend her party and I was unable to reach her by phone. I knew she had some minor health issues involving her digestive system, but they did not appear to be a cause for alarm. About an hour after the party finished, I received a phone call from my mother saying that she was unwell and in St Vincent's Hospital and asking that I come and see her. When I arrived at the hospital, my mother asked me to sit by her bed and told me that they had found advanced cancer of the duodenum. She looked me in the eyes when no one else was around and said, "Simon, they have given me twelve months." Hearing those words was like a punch in the stomach. My mother was just sixty-two years young at that time, vibrant and full of energy. I really believed that she had a lot more of life to live and I was shattered that hers too would be cut short.

Around that time my grandfather's health had also started to decline. He was nearing ninety and while his deterioration was not unexpected, his mind was so sharp and he was so alert that it was hard to reconcile it with his physical frailty. Over the next twelve months, I watched my mother undertake every possible cancer treatment in vain. Simultaneously, my grandfather just let nature take its course. My mother was confined to a wheelchair in her final months and my grandfather was mostly housebound. They were in constant communication and well aware of each other's predicament.

I looked after my mother as much as I could during that time and we spent many hours talking about the past and connecting on a deeper level than we had before. We spoke about my father, a topic that had been off-limits for many years. The pain of losing her true soulmate never diminished and she internalised those emotions until her dying day. We reminisced about the good times in Perth and generally focused on feel-good memories as a source of nostalgic comfort for both of us. I wanted to ask many more questions about the past, but it just didn't feel right at the time and now of course, I wish I had. Regardless, I have closure in the belief that she loved us very much and her parenting was simply from a different era and probably hard for my generation to understand and relate to.

On 21 October 2006, I was with my daughters at a Hi-5 concert and halfway through I received a phone call that my grandfather had passed away. I recall the last conversation I had with him only the day before, when through laboured breath he told me that he loved me. I knew the day was coming, but to actually lose the man you thought was larger than life was devastating.

The very next day the team in my office invited me in for a drink in his honour. That evening, I flew to Perth for my grandfather's funeral and flew straight back, not knowing how long my mum had. The day I got back from Perth was my elder daughter's birthday, exactly twelve months to the day that my mother was diagnosed. Despite fading in and out of consciousness and gasping for breath, I think she knew that it was my daughter's birthday. As midnight ticked over, she took her final breath as she lay in my sister's arms and mine.

Losing my grandfather and then my mother four days apart felt like a very bad dream and desperately surreal. My dear grandmother passed away three months after and, to this day, I wish that my grandparents and my mother had lived to meet my son.

The Hardest Day

I was told early on in my sentence that the hardest part of jail was the day you leave. Regardless, I romanticised about my release for years, making exciting plans in my head, coming up with new ideas in plotting my return, thinking about my family, where I would live, who I would be and the fact that I was pretty much starting life from scratch. My 'rebirth' was a daydream, an aspiration, a goal, that kept me going in jail and helped me through some of the hardest times. The reality of getting out, however, was very anticlimactic.

The morning of my fist day out, 31 January 2015, was spent with my kids eating, laughing and watching them set up my Facebook profile. We sat in a café in Willoughby for hours, even though it seemed like minutes. I remember looking at my children and imagining what it must have been like for them without a father for the past four years and the impact on their life including school, friends and their world in general. I oscillated between feelings of joy and the all too familiar immense guilt for letting them down.

Later that afternoon, some of my friends took me to Sydney's Bondi Beach so that I could put my feet in the ocean. As we then sat at the local RSL, a frightening sense of surreal reality suddenly engulfed me. I was completely overwhelmed by the notion of re-entering a world no longer familiar and restarting life. Facing my family, friends and especially those I had let down. Readjusting to life as a free man and finding my feet in the community. Surviving financially, making ends meet and providing for those I loved, not to mention accomplishing the dreams and ambitions I had created in jail. I found myself sitting there and drowning in the noise of life happening around me. My mind was spiralling with fear and uncertainty and it was totally petrifying.

I walked out of jail with nothing but the shirt on my back and had $100 to my name. I never considered some of the challenges I would face in my first few days of freedom. Should I buy a newspaper or a coffee? I can't afford both. Who should I call? Who would take my call? What would they say? I had no transport. I had no phone. My pre-jail clothes did not fit. How could I earn enough money to get on my feet? I wasn't even sure what my career opportunities looked like now that I had a criminal record.

It suddenly did not feel like a fresh start at all. It felt like I was miles behind the eight-ball. The routine of jail can be hypnotic and, although incredibly hard, it's also safe and predicable. How ironic that freedom was the more frightening option now, more so than I ever imagined.

One Step at a Time

In the early days after my release from jail, I stayed in some pre-arranged temporary accommodation. I hardly slept a wink during my first few nights alone. I was paranoid that at any moment the parole officers would knock on the door to take me back to jail. Walking the streets as a free man again was also disturbing. I was convinced, even though it was far from reality, that everyone was looking at me, thinking and knowing that I was a criminal. It would take me many months to shake that paranoia.

My first parole meeting happened to be on my second day out of jail. Walking into a parole office that soon after my release and being reminded of the consequences of any breach in parole was a stark reminder of days that I hoped would be well behind me. I think, however, that the meetings also gave me increased determination to keep moving forward. My parole conditions included fifteen strict rules that could not be breached, such as breaking the law in any way, other than traffic offences, staying at a pre-approved residence, undertaking random drug tests and not leaving the state of NSW. The most relevant to my crime was that I was not to engage in any activity, paid or non-paid, relating to the control of assets of other people or organisations. But most importantly, I was never to miss the monthly parole meeting.

Another condition of parole was to maintain gainful employment upon release. That suited me fine, as providing for my children and re-establishing as much of my independence as possible was absolutely critical. Fortunately, the premise of the jail work release program that I was participating in was that, upon release, the inmate had immediate transition into full-time employment. In my case, the transition into the workforce was maintaining my employment at OBK. Despite it not being a financially viable option in the long term, the idea of working for a non-profit and helping others felt like a good first step on the outside.

Working for OBK as a free man meant that the scope of my responsibilities expanded. I was now running corporate events and presented as a speaker on many occasions. The after-school volunteer program was also my responsibility and I was heavily involved in the operation of the Kitchen, seamlessly run by the general manager. I was now also working closely with the rabbi and his wife, the founders of OBK, and was quite surprised to be tasked by the rabbi to assist in the completion of his thesis to obtain his doctorate some twenty years in the making. I wonder if my jail-acquired qualifications in library and information services made me the right candidate to chip into his PHD.

Phoenix Rising Perhaps

An unwavering supporter and friend while in jail was a former colleague at SFG. One day he and his wife attended a children's party at OBK and he suggested that when I was ready to re-enter a semi-corporate environment, he and his business partner had a role just right for me. In addition to his offer, I was fortunate in that a number of other opportunities were presenting themselves at around the same time to resume corporate life. Despite my financial objectives, I felt very conflicted about returning to the corporate world too soon after my release. Lying low had felt more comfortable for the time being and I was quite enjoying a more altruistic line of work.

Following my conversation with my old colleague, however, I took a leap of faith and went for an interview with him and his partner to map out what a role for me in their company could look like. The opportunity ended up being very enticing because it involved entering a new industry yet again and as such, doing something entirely different. Furthermore, it also provided a chance to start connecting with old business contacts. We agreed on a role where my earning capacity was based on a fair base salary, as well as commission, and I started my new job in August 2015.

At first, my role involved selling LED lighting platforms to commercial clients. It entailed removing redundant and inefficient lighting to make way for new energy-efficient lighting platforms and attracting generous government incentives along the way. The incentives were in the form of a tradeable commodity and therefore determined the amount of commission on each deal. There was a sliding scale of incentive depending on the industry, be it retail, industrial or commercial.

I absolutely thrived in my new environment but, above all, I was elated that so many of the corporate doors of my past opened so easily and were ready to do business with me. The lighting business continued to grow over the next four years and I continued to not only focus on expanding our commercial client base, but also took the opportunity to get on the tools and embrace tradie life. One of the biggest lessons I learnt was the ability to move on from a deal that fell through. The reality of a discretionary sales-based role, with a fair share of competitors, meant that regardless of the effort and time put into winning the business, chances of a win were not a given. Here I was a forty-eight-year-old dog, once again learning new lessons and tricks in the big bad world.

In 2019, my employers recognised an opportunity to expand the business operations to include fire compliance. It effectively enabled us to offer clients a full lighting, electrical and fire compliance solution. Once again, the chance arose for me to take on the challenge of learning yet another trade. Segueing into the fire industry enabled me to roll all the skills

I had acquired over my entire career into a new profession. I am now studying further to gain a variety of qualifications and advance my industry standing.

You never know what is around the corner, but I really love working in the fire industry. Every day is a new location, a new challenge and a new opportunity to utilise my knowledge. No two days in fire are the same. I am now in the role of chief investigator, as a qualified and accredited fire certifier, which not only allows me to continue doing what I really like, but I also get to teach and mentor a team of fire technicians as the business grows. The role also enables me to advise on implementing systems and processes to optimise our backend operations. Who would have thought that I would find my feet and be so fulfilled on so many levels wearing hi-viz, steel caps and my tool belt. A far cry from my corporate attire of a past life.

Becoming a Father Again

I walked into jail a married, hands-on father of three children and walked out a single father, not really knowing what that would actually look like. The logistics of separate living arrangements, custody, access, visitation and child support were yet to be determined pieces of the post jail life puzzle. How would my children perceive me? Would they listen and follow my parenting despite such a long absence? Could I show them how much I loved and missed them? Could I rebuild their respect and any standing as a role model? Would my return affect their social life or will there be consequences of their father having been to jail? And most importantly, how would my release impact my children's overall well-being and what could I do to provide the best support and stability?

My integration into their world was understandably cautious and measured. It started with having the children stay with me two nights a week for the first few months. Once trust and familiarity were established, we moved to an arrangement where they were with me five days a fortnight. Despite my initial trepidation as to how I would fit into their life, I was surprised at how welcoming the general parent community was towards me and I genuinely felt that many were happy that my children had a father figure again.

The first parent-teacher evening for each of my children was an absolute highlight. Just being able to go and participate in their life once more was a such a milestone. I almost could not have cared what the teachers had to say at that point. I was just happy to be there. Attending sports carnivals, after-school activities, play dates and parties were now an absolute treat and, while they might have been mundane to some, unsurprisingly, they were very enjoyable for me.

Sharing custody of my children gave me the incredible high of parenting and then the low and empty feeling when they were not with me. At that time, I was renting a nice apartment in St Ives with more than enough room for my kids to have their own space and certainly having friends over, especially as my girls were becoming teenagers and their social circles were increasingly more important. Our favourite family pastime was going to the football together. We never missed a home game of our precious Roosters.

During this time, I would think of the words that the judge had said on a number of occasions during my trial. "Simon, for a man who grew up without a father and made it clear that you would never put your children in a position to be without a father, the reality is your children will now not have you around for some time." Of all the assertions I heard during the entire criminal proceedings, that statement stuck with me the most and definitely fuelled my guilt. The fact that I had not been there for them for years was gut-wrenching enough. Given my childhood, however, the reality that I destined my children to a similar fate presented an additional level of sorrow.

My children and I did not discuss the past or my time in jail too much. There was the occasional question of curiosity, but I believe that we all instinctively drifted towards picking up where we left off and living as normally as possible. I smile when I think about my naivety with regard to social media and the fun that we had setting up my social and LinkedIn profiles. When I was first incarcerated, the world was up to an iPhone 3 and app development was in its infancy. Once I came out, we were at iPhone 6 and there was an app for most things.

For the next few years, I was walking a fine line of trying to be a good parent and establish boundaries and guidance accordingly, while feeling an overwhelming need to please my children, and indeed many around me, which of course drove me to overcompensate and be agreeable, even if to my own detriment. It took me a long time to acknowledge that such an approach was ill-fated and ultimately did not serve anyone's best interest. Boundaries are really the foundations of respect, be it in parenting, business or life. And boundaries are imperative to the success of any relationship regardless of who the parties are. And if one oversteps those boundaries, it's a long journey back.

In the case of the father and son dynamic, I gravitated towards trying to replicate the father and son relationship that I experienced in my early childhood and subsequently missed out on. As an obvious starting point, I encouraged my son to choose a sport of interest so that we could embrace it together. As sporty as I had always been, my son chose the one sport that although I enjoyed to watch have never actually played. The quintessential Australian sport of cricket. True to the pleaser within, I purchased a full cricket kit with all the bells and whistles so he could join the local cricket club. Unfortunately, I later realised that he only chose the sport as his friends were in the team and, while he relished the social aspect, he did not really care for the game, resulting in our cricket journey lasting one season. As luck would have it, an old school friend of mine was collecting second-hand cricket gear to send to impoverished communities overseas, so at least the gear was not purchased in vain.

I came to realise that my son's talent and interest was more on the creative side and team sport was not high on the radar. I was happy to abandon the dialogue around sport, because of the absolute joy that I had in seeing him put his inventiveness into action. To this day, his creative accomplishments are well ahead of his years and I am incredibly proud of his talent, as well as general empathy and demeanour in his world.

As one would imagine, I really wanted to get parenting right the second time around. My priority was to be consistent, loving and there for my children when I was needed. To rebuild my relationship with them was my driving force. There have been many twists and turns in that journey since my release and I have learnt that regardless of the intent, the outcome is not a given. The lesson for me, however, is that I can only focus on what I can control and must let go of what I can't. And today, I am at relative peace with that.

Setbacks

Unless court-ordered, or due to a mental health diagnosis while in custody, there are no structured post jail mental health programs or services. That places the onus on the newly released inmate to take their well-being into their own hands. Of course, it is not a foolproof solution as it relies on self-diagnosis, self-awareness and access to mental health services. In many cases the cost of seeking help is also often prohibitive. That should really come as no surprise in view of the lack of non-essential services on the inside. I suspect that given that there is no political advantage or votes to be gained for addressing the mental health and well-being of criminals, many inmates fall through the gap of post jail assessment and care to assist their adjustment to life on the outside.

In my case, I was overwhelmed by my own expectations to reinvent myself in part fuelled by my remorse but also the ever-present external pressures. My life quickly became a pinball machine and I was the pinball. It was a never-ending cycle of trying to cover every base and tick every box. In hindsight, I was unable to say no, regardless of the impact on me. I felt an instinctive obligation to become a pleaser, perhaps as a method of redemption. My desire to rise from the shame was one of my biggest challenges. I am convinced that this is not a unique predicament for newly released inmates seeking to rebuild and resume their life.

My day-to-day life became a matter of keeping my head above water. On reflection, I know that I had not properly processed or dealt with my years in jail. In fact, quite often I would stop dead in my tracks wondering who I was or what I actually wanted from life, other than being with my children of course. I had no concept of what else made me happy, how to do anything to bring me joy or how to be at peace. Certainly, drinking in any capacity, smoking or taking recreational drugs were not an option, as I had never enjoyed them at all.

About two years after my release, I was driving to work one day and the next thing I recall is being awake in a hospital bed. I had no idea where I was, what was wrong with me, what day it was and how I got there. I saw a drip in my arm and monitoring devices stuck to my chest. I was very groggy and not thinking clearly. I don't remember if it was a nurse or a doctor who asked me if I knew where I was, who I was or whether I was hungry and thirsty. The only real question I could answer is who I was.

I'm unsure of the sequence of events that followed or how long it took me to be fully lucid again, but I remember the nurse and doctor telling me that they believed me to have been missing for about a week, that my vitals were very unstable and that I needed to remain in hospital. I was then informed that I would be assessed by the psychiatric registrar and moved to the adult mental health unit. I was completely shocked and in disbelief and kept asking the doctor whether I was crazy and if something was wrong with me. At that stage, the doctor indicated that it seemed that I had some kind of breakdown, but it would have to be diagnosed and assessed within the mental health unit. I remember asking for my phone so that I could call my children. However, I have no recollection of what device I was given, or who in my family I spoke to first.

I was in the emergency ward of a public hospital and during the course of the hours it took to be transferred, I was slowly regaining my senses. At some point, I had my mobile phone in hand and turned it on to an avalanche of messages by people who had been trying to contact me. I had no idea of the social tsunami that I had created and as I was reading and listening to countless messages, I was completely overwhelmed yet totally confused as to how I got into the situation. I eventually spoke to a number of family and friends to try and piece together what had happened to me and to let them know that I was safe. After confirming whether I was okay, every person I spoke to immediately told me that no one knew where I was and that I had been missing for a week. In addition, everyone had been working together to find me.

I was soon moved to a psychiatric observation unit and looked after by the acute mental health team. There was no immediate diagnosis and while I don't know who came to visit me first, I remember a number of people coming and bringing me clothing and personal items.

In the ensuing days, I was moved to the long care adult mental health unit within Hornsby Public Hospital, where a number of members of the mental health team interviewed me to try and establish what had happened. From that point onwards, only my close friends came to see me, perhaps unsurprisingly the same people who had regularly visited me in jail.

Being in a secure mental health facility was eerily similar to jail. The way that food was served, medication dispensed, meals delivered and even the way the rooms were set up. When I spoke to the mental health team to explain that I was increasingly uncomfortable, they told me that I could be going through a PTSD-related episode. The daily cycle of doctors and various therapies, however, were not conclusive in explaining how I ended up MIA for a week.

As the next step, the mental health team informed me that they contacted some of the mental health professionals who I had been examined by during my legal proceedings to further understand my mental health history. After multiple daily psychiatric sessions and also exploring my twenty-four-hour blackout that occurred years earlier, just before my sentencing, the resident psychiatrist concluded that I had experienced a dissociative fugue episode. As it was explained to me, when it presents itself, the mind completely shuts down and the body becomes a shell in survival mode. I was told that one of the most famous cases of this condition was experienced by Agatha Christie. After supporting her husband for many years, he was unfaithful and unkind and left her by running off with his mistress. She experienced a period of out-of-body amnesia induced by stress which effectively rendered her in a trance for eleven days. So much so, that she took a fake name, went on a trip, stayed in a hotel and did not recognise her own photograph in newspapers reporting her disappearance.

Upon learning the diagnosis, my first reaction was one of fear that it could be a recurring event. I really wanted to understand the trigger and the signs that I needed to look out for should such a state present itself again. I was advised that the signs would be similar to someone suffering severe depression, including not wanting to get out of bed, lacking motivation for daily routine, general fatigue, loss of appetite and no interest in any form of self-care. Sure enough, in the lead-up to my disappearance, I remember losing complete motivation for my daily exercise regime and not being hungry at all. The doctor recommended that I start taking anti-anxiety medication to stabilise my anxiety and told me that it would take up to six weeks for full efficacy. I started the medication in hospital and for the rest of my week's stay went through the motions required of me, keen to get out as soon as possible and escape the overwhelming reminder of jail.

When I think back on that time in hospital, I can't help but reflect on the similarities and stark differences between a mental health hospital and jail. The physical confinement of both, one due to choices in life and governed with discipline, the other as a result of ill health and administered, seemingly, with one's best interests at heart. On the subject of best interests, during the time I was missing, my trusted friend Gerry set up a Go Fund Me campaign to raise money to provide financial assistance. When I later found out about it in hospital, I was overwhelmed with appreciation, but it was equally humiliating. To this day, I am too uncomfortable to see who supported the fund. However, I am deeply grateful for the outpouring of community support. I allowed the trustee of the fund to disperse all moneys on my behalf in the most responsible way that he saw fit as I felt that it was the morally right thing to do.

And Life Goes On

To my relief, I was out of hospital without any further incidents and hastily returned to my life. I continued to take the prescribed anti-anxiety medication and only saw the doctor for script renewal and did not seek further psychiatric help. Over the next few months, the medication's side effects were really starting to weigh me down. I lacked energy, libido and drive, and felt quite ordinary and not myself. As the state continued, I was increasingly worried that my condition might deteriorate and would render me unwell again. Consequently, I made the decision to voluntarily check myself back into the Hornsby Hospital for mental health maintenance. While I was there and probably thanks to my medication, I did not experience the jail triggers of last time. The mental health team, however, determined that the particular medication was not suited to manage my mental health. Therefore, it was recommended that over the forthcoming weeks, I slowly reduce my dose and wean off the medication altogether. Again, other than the medical aspect of my treatment, I did not embrace any other therapeutic intervention, mainly because I felt that my main problem was being on the medication in the first place. After a few days, I checked out and resumed life, waiting for the effects of the medication to subside.

Sure enough, within a few weeks I felt far more lucid and back to my normal state. Life at the time was quite busy with interstate and overseas visitors, a fair amount of travel for work and, in my spare time, I tried to reignite my love for reading and, as always, continued my nightly twenty-minute exercise regime to clear and settle my mind. I did everything that I could to maintain my equilibrium and therefore keep my mental health in check and my anxiety at bay.

Almost a year after the mental health maintenance visit, I ignored some red flags creeping into my life once more. I was still working in the same job and life in general was stable, yet it felt like I was not achieving anything and was barely keeping my head above water. I lost the drive to exercise and the energy to engage socially, and felt a real sense of detachment from myself and the world around me. And as I was to later find out, what came next was another complete mental shutdown. I was driving around on a work day and have no recall of the next week of my life. Whether I ate, slept, drank, where I was or how I existed. I was located wandering on the Northern Beaches in a disoriented state and apparently could barely communicate.

I was taken to Hornsby Hospital once more and treated by the medical team much like the previous time. Although it was the same process of consultations, therapies and diagnosis, there were two significant developments this time around. The first was that I verbalised to my doctors and therapists that I had been sexually assaulted and that I had been hiding and carrying it ever since. It's hard to describe how I felt when

I finally said what had happened out loud. The enormous weight that had lifted, the sense of relief and the emotion that came with it all were completely overwhelming.

The other important progress during this stay was a connection that I made with an occupational therapist. I credit this man with giving me a real breakthrough in my treatment, because for the first time on my entire mental health journey, I felt that someone was offering a strategy for getting well instead of laying too much emphasis on the diagnosis. His first question that set the tone for all our sessions was simply "Simon, when was the last time you did something for yourself?" I was silent not only because I was dumbstruck by what seemed a rather unsophisticated approach, but also because I actually could not remember. And as we further explored the topic, it became evident that so many people fall into the trap of existing in a life of routine as opposed to living a life of enjoyment and purpose. Two people can live with the same challenges, adversities, highs and successes, but the way they live through it all is what makes all the difference.

In my case, it was clear that I undertook almost everything in my life from a standpoint of 'I must'. Even exercising regularly came from a place of routine, rather than enjoyment and much needed release. I had no concept of doing anything for me and I certainly did not practise taking pleasure in the small things throughout my day. It's an ever-so-slight mindset shift, with a huge upside if one can master it and apply it to everyday life. As an example, for me, my morning coffee is about the experience of smelling, tasting and appraising my double espresso, rather than just seeing it as a hit of caffeine.

For the rest of my stay in hospital, I spent a few hours a day with the occupational therapist, and also a social worker, focusing on understanding and embracing some of the fundamental principles of what I learnt to be positive psychology. Although it's by no means rocket science, it does require discipline and an investment in oneself. And it takes practice to appreciate and embrace the fine line between going through the motions of life and being truly present in the moment and valuing it.

I realised that focusing on self-compassion, facing fears and changing the narrative around day-to-day life has the potential to pay major dividends in life, a crucial one being that they underpin my resilience. And with resilience comes the capacity to better deal with all aspects of life and, most importantly, the ability to bounce back from life's challenges.

I did not expect the simplest treatment method to be the one that started my healing and my road to better mental health. Unsurprisingly, during my hospital stay, the doctors also reconfirmed their initial diagnosis of PTSD resulting from my experiences in jail. I am therefore acutely aware that managing my well-being is an ongoing process and am committed to practise my strategies every day.

Friend or Foe

I was often reminded on the inside that, no matter what I did once I was a free man, there would be those that will never break bread with me again and will always look out for that chink in my armour. Then there would be those, I was told, who would inevitably believe that I should live my life out with my head held low. And for a long time, I was probably resigned to doing just that. But that has changed, because it simply has to or what's the point? At some stage, you have to choose to forgive yourself and hope that those who matter also forgive you. I have chosen to move forward and to do my best to thrive and only those who understand that belong in my world. I feel extremely lucky for my close circle of support and have immense gratitude and love for those friends and family who did not waver in their friendship throughout the years.

Along the way, I have also come to realise that irrespective of the crime, remorse, physical or mental state, many in society do regard those who have 'done time' as persona non grata. Further, there are many challenges in settling back into life after release, and day-to-day freedoms take time to be granted. They include difficulty in getting life, car and general insurance, overseas travel, financial credit and even simply getting gainful employment where a police check is often required. In my case, even nine years down the track, I continue to encounter difficulties in daily life. That is the unfortunate reality for so many who, even after having done their time, are faced with the uphill battle to start afresh in a largely unforgiving world.

I have lost count of the number of people who have said that I should write a book about my journey. I never knew what shape it would take, how I would start and if I even had the resources or headspace to make it happen. But the idea of telling my side of events was always something I knew I needed to do. Because while the headlines of what happened are true, a great many falsities have also been attached to what transpired. And while I do not lose any sleep these days over what people might think of my past, it is my story to own.

And then in early 2021 and purely by chance, I met my co-conspirator, a remarkably inspiring and exceptional human. We immediately connected and she swiftly broke down my walls without judgement and with a hunger to know more. She also quickly became the unstoppable force that drove this book to reality. Due to COVID lockdowns and our heavy work and life commitments, writing took place in whatever location was possible, be it parks, pubs or bus stops when it rained. The fact that at times we bumped into people related to the subject matter we were writing about was also quite uncanny. I really can't imagine having gone through the process with anyone else. I am still surprised at how relatively straightforward it has been, no doubt made so by enormous trust on both sides and the fact that she was the one noting my stream of consciousness and then of course had to make sense of it all.

The months of writing and recounting my journey has also reminded me of all the remarkable, compassionate and colourful souls that I have had the fortune to cross paths with and have in my world. Many are referred to in this book but there are many more in my heart.

Mirror Mirror

My years in jail provided ample time to reflect and hold myself accountable against the values that guided my upbringing. It is soul-destroying to admit that I am grateful that the role models of these principles were not around to witness the choices I made or the subsequent twists and turns of my life. I would also love to say that I walked out of jail a transformed man. A man who is rehabilitated and ready to tackle the world with integrity and authenticity. I think that's what society and the community would expect. If I was an observer, I would too. Surely, that would, at least in part, be the outcome of doing time.

I can't speak for others, but for me, time on the inside was, in part, about enduring the consequence of my wrongdoing. Deservedly, it also served to accustom me to unrelenting feelings of shame, guilt and self-disdain. But did my crime and the price I paid really make me a better man? No, I do not think so at all. I would say a law-abiding man, absolutely. A deeply sorry man, unquestionably. But I now see that I made little progress in facing the real me. Owning who that person is, warts and all. Recognising my actions, my drivers, my weaknesses. I walked out of jail without even scratching the surface of why I am the way I am and I was happy not to face any of that, especially in the early years of freedom. Life was complicated enough and it was challenging to keep it all together. But perhaps also because deep down I knew that maybe that's when the real work would begin.

And so it is fair to say that I have spent the past nine years living a life that is far from authentic or aligned with the version of me that would make me proud. That is not to say that I have not been a good or kind person or a better person in general. Not at all. However, I have not been able to move past my pattern of the pleaser, preoccupied with approval. I wanted to be the hero. Because anything less was failure. To be validated, liked and valued was my drug, my dependency.

Unfortunately, not even jail, personal loss or remorse has been able to stop me from spiralling into a world of pretence from time to time. Convincing people around me that everything was fine, that I had the means, that I was nailing life and that I was on the right track was routine. I mostly even convinced myself. I did not want to let anyone down. Certainly not again. And living a life where I had all the answers became a habit I could not shake. And while I have never acted unlawfully since my crime, I have, over the years, continued to get myself into situations of 'over promise and under deliver', only to ultimately unravel and self-destruct when it all became too hard. Followed by the need to disappear. For ever.

Looking back, a version of what I have just described must have been my modus operandi for as long as I can remember. I reflected not long ago about how much I used to hate being called charming, funny and someone who had a knack for being a 'Mr Fix It'. How ironic. To be fair, I used those talents to my advantage too. But the reality of what those attributes could have done, and have done, to me and to those in my world was not something that I had ever truly tackled. Until hopefully now.

I am currently hard at work. On me. And it's not pretty. And I imagine it will be tough. But it's real. And in a way, incredibly liberating. Perhaps foremost because being a chameleon is so exhausting. So are guilt and sorrow. I accept that regardless of any future personal progress and growth, my regret will mark the rest of my life. And that foremost includes those I have wronged or let down. Many are no longer in my life. However, I'm incredibly lucky to say that many still are. Thank you for sticking by me. I am tempted to tell you not to worry and that it will be fine.

But I won't pretend to know. All I know is that I have a plan and best intentions. But that chapter is yet to be.

www.ingramcontent.com/pod-product-compliance
Lightning Source LLC
Chambersburg PA
CBHW030550080526
44585CB00012B/330